VALUING PEOPLE TO CREATE VALUE

An Innovative Approach to Leveraging Motivation at Work

Hervé Mathe
Xavier Pavie
Marwyn O'Keeffe

ESSEC Business School, Paris-Singapore

World Scientific

NEW JERSEY · LONDON · SINGAPORE · BEIJING · SHANGHAI · HONG KONG · TAIPEI · CHENNAI

Published by

World Scientific Publishing Co. Pte. Ltd.

5 Toh Tuck Link, Singapore 596224

USA office: 27 Warren Street, Suite 401-402, Hackensack, NJ 07601

UK office: 57 Shelton Street, Covent Garden, London WC2H 9HE

British Library Cataloguing-in-Publication Data
A catalogue record for this book is available from the British Library.

VALUING PEOPLE TO CREATE VALUE
An Innovative Approach to Leveraging Motivation at Work

ISBN-13 978-981-4365-06-2
ISBN-10 981-4365-06-8

In-house Editor: Sandhya Venkatesh

Typeset by Stallion Press
Email: enquiries@stallionpress.com

Printed in Singapore.

VALUING PEOPLE TO CREATE VALUE

An Innovative Approach to Leveraging Motivation at Work

CONTENTS

Chapter 1

INTRODUCTION

A motivated workforce is a valuable driver of business success. People who care about and take a vested interest in the performance of their organisation play a pivotal role in leveraging its capacity to thrive in a competitive global marketplace. Yet, motivation is an elusive concept; it is not a tangible process, nor does it correspond to a one-size-fits-all model. What is motivation precisely, and how can it be developed or inspired in the workplace? This book focuses on motivational approaches drawn from a broad qualitative sample of today's most successful and innovative organisations worldwide. Based on the findings from these approaches, we have defined an innovative *Motivation Spectrum*, which can be adapted to optimally leverage motivation in the workforce; the aim is to bring out the best in employees for enhancing organisational and individual value. Each organisation takes a unique and innovative approach to motivation; yet, common to all is the importance placed on reciprocating the value that employees bring to the organisation. Taking an interest in their individual needs and aspirations is a key and fundamental parameter for leveraging sustainable motivation at work.

1.1. The Roots of Motivation

The term 'motivation' derives from the Latin word for movement, *movere.* The verb 'to motivate' first gained currency in the English language around the year 1860, and was defined as 'to stimulate toward action' implying the stimulation of *movement.* Motivation is the force that causes us to go to work every day; it is the energy that fuels our performance; it explains why our performance varies from one day to another, or why we switch from one task to another; it underpins our choices at work and our drive to succeed.

From Human Motivation...

We can trace the study of motivation as far back as the Greek philosophers. Plato believed that man's ability to set goals for himself made his choice of the goal the chief determinant of his subsequent course of action, the idea that human behaviour is inherently purposeful. The concept of goal-directed behaviour is echoed by the ancient Greek concept of hedonism, that humans seek to pursue pleasure and to avoid pain, and remained an influential concept for 20th century thinkers.[1] At the beginning of the 20th century, Tolman developed his theory of purposive behaviour, with much of his studies examining motivated behaviour in animals, in an effort to understand human behaviour.[2] Tolman's discovery that rats solve mazes faster when hungry indeed helped to further unravel the puzzle of motivation, yet we were at that time a long way from fully understanding the more complex nature of *human* motivation.

... To Motivation at Work...

Explorations of the concept of motivation abound in the last century, from studies of human motivation in a universal sense to the more specific subject of motivating people at work. Throughout the 20th century, many social scientists studying motivation in parallel used very different approaches. Frederick Taylor introduced the concept of scientific management at the beginning of the 20th century to a world that was eager for progress and becoming increasingly industrial. A revolutionary concept at the time, in retrospect it was argued that Taylorism ignored the human side of motivation. His scientific approach to motivation was for a time successful with significant increases in productivity; yet, it ultimately revealed its limits in the monotony created by task repetition and the lack of concern for human needs.[3]

---

[1] Bolles, RC (1967). *Theory of Motivation.* New York: Harper & Row.
[2] Tolman, EC (1932). *Purposive Behavior in Animals and Men.* New York: Century Co.
[3] Hartness, J (1912). *The Human Factor in Works Management.* New York and London: McGraw-Hill.

... To Positive Motivation for Organisational Performance ...

As an antidote to the coercive approach to motivation, many theorists responded with a decidedly more humane position. Douglas McGregor published *The Human Side of Enterprise* in 1960 in which he advocated a form of management that entrusted employees with responsibility and provided opportunities for progression; otherwise, McGregor argued, the force of management would inevitably breed employee counterforce.[4] One of the most impactful changes that occurred in the development of motivation over the last century was the move away from a concept of motivation that viewed humans as malleable and exploitable, like cogs in a machine or just another input in the system.

One particular motivation study demonstrates the often enigmatic quality of motivation, but nevertheless leaves us with a lesson to remember. Elton Mayo ran his famous Hawthorne factory experiments in 1955. When studying the effect of improved lighting conditions on productivity in the factory, Mayo found that workers' productivity rose when he turned on the lights and rose higher still when he turned them off. It was concluded that the mere act of paying attention to workers' needs and showing an interest in them was inherently motivating.[5]

Yet, with the wealth of theories of motivation at our disposition, are we any closer to understanding motivation at work today? One point is certain — treating workers with a respect for the value they bring to the organisation remains as valid a lesson today as it did in 1955. In the contemporary business environment, the link between individual motivation and organisational performance is patently clear, and initiatives to support employee engagement and positive motivation have become a widespread practice.

1.2.　What is Motivation at Work?

Defining Motivation ...

Motivation is an internal energy stimulated by the drive to attain goals to satisfy a set of individual needs and values. Motivation initiates an individual's choice of behaviour and determines its form and direction, intensity of effort, and persistence over time.

---

[4] McGregor, D (1960). *The Human Side of Enterprise*. New York: McGraw-Hill.

[5] Trahair, R (2005). *Elton Mayo: The Humanist Temper*. London: Transaction Publishers.

Motivation *at work* is the ability of the organisation to stimulate a person's motivation to wilfully strive towards the achievement of organisational goals by providing opportunities to fulfil individual needs.

What about satisfaction, well-being, and engagement? Motivation at work is an overarching notion that encompasses nuanced realities: satisfaction and well-being are undeniably essential components of employee motivation; engagement is a useful concept to designate a high level of involvement and a commitment to the success of the company, i.e., the willingness to 'go the extra mile' for the organisation. By approaching motivation in the right way, a motivated workforce will be both engaged and satisfied.

1.3.   A Motivated Workforce is a Key Driver of Business Success

Motivation remains an elusive concept. To understand motivation, one must understand human nature itself and touch upon several disciplines. Thus the subject of motivation is often not clearly understood and it is difficult to be put in practice. Yet in today's hypercompetitive marketplace, understanding what fosters and advances employee motivation is vital as it drives organisational performance. People who care about and take a vested interest in the performance of their organisation play a pivotal role in leveraging its capacity to succeed in a global world.

PART 1

THE FOUNDATIONS OF MOTIVATION
AT WORK

The three chapters in Part 1 — the Building Blocks, the Processes and the Architecture of Motivation at Work — are designed to collectively explain motivation at work. They are based on the theoretical explorations of social scientists over the past 150 years during which time vastly different types of theories about motivation were developed. A historical classification would not be useful for tracing the development of motivation because similar theories were developed at opposite ends of the same century and are more useful when examined together. Hence, we have decided to classify the theories under three umbrella categories in order to best understand the concept of motivation and what it means today. Some of the theories are timeless, while others belong in the past; we have selected those that are still to a large extent valid today and which collectively help us to understand motivation at work.

We begin with an exploration of the Building Blocks of Motivation at Work in Chapter 1 — the theories focusing on human needs. A set of fundamental needs lie at the root of human behaviour and act as a stimulus to drive behaviour at work. This chapter explores the different theories pertaining to human needs.

Yet, needs alone do not entirely explain the process of motivation; humans, being cognitively advanced and capable of rational decision-making, are each day faced with choices: which task to pursue or how much energy to exert. The way in which we make choices depends on other factors such as the expectancy of whether one will succeed or not, the value one places on a reward or outcome; and the lessons from past experience. All of these cognitive processes are explored in Chapter 3, The Processes of Motivation at Work.

Finally, in Chapter 4, the Architecture of Motivation at Work, we examine the overarching or underlying moderators that impact motivation: the supportive framework, the culture or the stage of an employee's life. These factors tell us that motivation is not a one-size-fits-all concept; it has to be moulded to fit the person, the organisation and the goals.

Chapter 2

THE BUILDING BLOCKS OF MOTIVATION AT WORK

Individual needs represent the basic building blocks in the whole process of motivation at work. Needs are internal motives or impulses that act as a stimulus for action and make certain outcomes appear attractive. While we are first and foremost driven by a need to satisfy primary needs such as food and security, we also look for satisfaction of the more abstract higher-level needs of esteem and fulfilment; these needs stimulate our behaviour at work and form the building blocks of motivated behaviour.

The central concept of this chapter is the idea that a set of fundamental needs lie at the root of human behaviour and act as a stimulus to drive behaviour. Human needs represent a driver of human behaviour in all aspects of life; they are the reason why people go to work, why some people complete tasks faster or more efficiently than others and why different people are attracted to different types of jobs or aspire to different goals.

We should consider the need motivation models and their implications collectively: beginning with Maslow's hierarchy of needs, each subsequent model takes a different angle or contributes ancillary elements to the understanding of motivation at work. With many of the theories building upon or modifying a previous model to enlarge the perspective, it is thus useful to see the full panorama of theories in order to fully comprehend the way in which needs drive people to work.

The universality of the motivational models in this 'building blocks' chapter should also be noted; human needs are common to employees across all cultures, working climates and generations. And while there are certain elements of each theory whose validity has been questioned over time, there are salient points in each model to learn about motivation at work for motivating employees in the contemporary working environment.

2.1. Introduction to Human Needs

Most models of motivation are underpinned by the assumption that behaviour is directed towards the satisfaction of needs or goals.[1] These needs represent internal motives or impulses that act as an incitement to action. Specifically, a need can be defined as an internal state that makes certain outcomes appear attractive. An unsatisfied need creates a state of disequilibrium within the individual, which in turn stimulates certain drives. These drives generate a search behaviour to find particular goals that, if attained, will satisfy the need and re-establish the equilibrium. This is precisely what drives people's efforts and actions at work.[2]

In the workplace, the employee's actions are guided by efforts to satisfy internal needs; these efforts must coincide with the organisational goals in order for the employee's actions to result in a desired performance or productivity for the organisation. For instance, an employee may commit to the completion of an organisational project because he or she will also receive recognition and gain respect for himself or herself.

The understanding of human needs, and their place in the working environment, was greatly advanced by the eponymous model of human needs developed by Abraham Maslow in 1943. It remains to this day a referential theory for understanding the concept of motivation at work and represents the foundation on which many contemporary theories were developed.

2.1.1. *Glossary of Key Definitions for 'The Building Blocks of Motivation at Work'*

Need: A lack of something wanted or deemed necessary; creates an internal stimulus or motive for action towards the satisfaction of the need.

Primary Needs: The basic physiological drives such as breathing, hunger, shelter, love, safety, security, friendship, etc., many of which are directly dependent on a person's physical survival or wellness.

---

[1]Vroom, VH and EL Deci (1970). *Management and Motivation*. Baltimore: Penguin Education.
[2]Robbins, SP and DA DeCenzo (2008). *Fundamentals of Management: Essential Concepts and Applications*. New Jersey: Pearson Prentice Hall.

Higher-order Needs: These are more abstract, psychological desires for personal growth, esteem and self-fulfilment or self-actualisation. These needs are depicted in the higher levels of Maslow's hierarchy of needs.

Intrinsic Motivation: Intrinsic motivation in the working environment involves employees doing an activity because they find it interesting and derive spontaneous satisfaction from the activity itself. Intrinsic motivation comes from higher-order needs such as self-fulfilment, self-determination or the need for competency.

Extrinsic Motivation: Extrinsic motivation in the work context entails an instrumentality between the activity and consequences that are separate to the task itself, such as tangible, contingent or verbal rewards.

Self-determination: To be self-determining means an employee experiences a sense of choice in initiating and regulating his or her actions. It is the need to feel capable of choosing, to feel empowered and to be responsible for one's own behaviour as much as possible.

2.2. Overview of the Chapter

Commencing with the hierarchy of needs, we look at why Abraham Maslow ranked the full range of human needs into five categories, with the highest priority needs at the bottom. We then examine Alderfer's existence-relatedness-growth (ERG) model introduced over 20 years later, based on three fundamental categories of needs. Designed specifically for the working environment, Alderfer's model is a reinvention of the Maslow hierarchy that emphasises the idea that different needs come into play simultaneously and do not always follow the sequence of a hierarchy (Figure 2.1).

Subsequently we examine Herzberg's two-factor theory: Herzberg introduced the idea that hygiene needs, such as working conditions or supervision, have the greatest impact on demotivation when these hygiene needs are deemed unsatisfactory by the employee. Yet, once satisfied, they do not have a significant impact on motivation. He argued that 'motivators' were psychological factors such as awards, recognition and opportunities for growth.

We then focus more closely on higher-order needs; these are more abstract and psychological in nature. We first examine self-determination, the idea that people should not feel controlled or coerced into work tasks. This was introduced by Deci and Ryan who focused on the motivational

Valuing People to Create Value

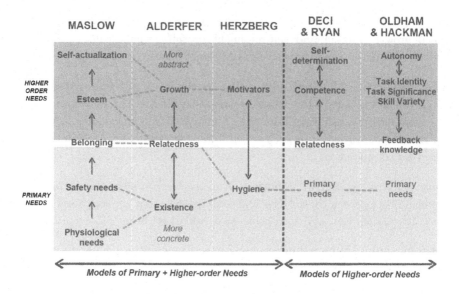

Figure 2.1   Overview of the need motivation theories.

effect of psychological needs, correlating with Maslow's concept of self-actualisation. We then return to Herzberg who delves deeper into the motivational capacity of higher-order needs through the concept of job enrichment. Finally, we look at another concept of motivation by higher-order needs: Hackman and Oldham's Job Characteristics Theory. This will bring us to the end of our exploration of needs at the heart of human motivation at work.

2.3.   Motivation by Primary and Higher-Order Needs

If we examine motivation at its most basic level in humans and animals, we observe that we are all primarily and instinctively motivated or driven to satisfy survival needs such as those for food, shelter and reproduction. Once these 'primary needs' are met, our priorities change and we become motivated to satisfy psychological needs, termed 'higher-order needs', which represent a drive for needs such as growth, esteem and fulfilment.

Primary needs are the basic human physiological drives such as breathing, hunger, shelter, love, safety, security, friendship, etc., many of which are dependent on a person's physical survival. Higher-order needs represent more abstract, psychological desires for personal growth, esteem and self-fulfilment or self-actualisation. These needs are depicted in the higher levels of Maslow's hierarchy of needs.

How do needs translate into employee motivation in a work environment? Essentially, the employee is first and foremost driven by a need to work for a salary or payment derived from a necessity to ensure shelter, food, among others. Evidently, the provision of a salary does not suffice to ensure the employee's motivation; a series of other needs come into play in the form of higher-order needs.

As we move from primary to higher-order needs, the articulation of the need becomes progressively more abstract, and accordingly more difficult to satisfy. It is precisely this inherent complexity that renders higher-order needs as more powerful 'motivators'; in a sense, higher-order needs are never absolutely satisfied and it is this drive to continually acquire knowledge, to grow and to progress that sets in motion the employee's long-term pursuit of need satisfaction, and accordingly the motivation at work. Remember that it is precisely the drive to satisfy a need that creates motivation, and a satisfied need no longer motivates. In other words, the drive to satisfy higher-order needs explains an individual's desire to progress within the organisation, or if necessary, to change jobs if greater opportunities or more interesting work are offered elsewhere.

On a worldwide level, the maturity and advancement of a country may affect the type of needs of the workforce; for instance, in a developing country, the need for food and security may be more pressing than in a developed country in the Western world. Even within a country, there will be great variation in terms of the importance of needs across different social groups. Needs for food, shelter and basic physiological factors do not always represent a driving force for human motivation. Nevertheless, changes in circumstances can imply a change in needs, and primary needs may come into play at various stages in an employee's lifetime.[3]

2.3.1. *A Hierarchy of Needs*

Developed by Abraham Maslow (1943).

Overview

Abraham Maslow presented the concept that not only are there many human needs, ranging from basic physiological drives such as hunger to a

---

[3]Hackman, J Richard and E Lawlor (1971). Employee reactions to job characteristics. *Journal of Applied Psychology*, 55, 259–286.

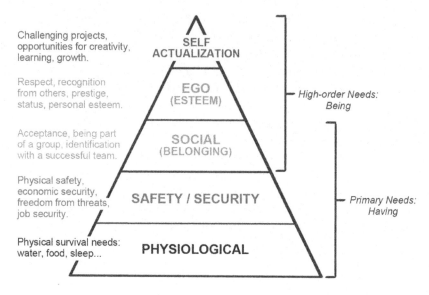

Adapted from Maslow (1943) by ESSEC ISIS

Figure 2.2   The hierarchy of needs.

more abstract desire for self-actualisation, but also that they are arranged in a hierarchy whereby the primary needs must to a large degree be satisfied before higher-order needs come into play (Figure 2.2).[4]

Maslow put forward the idea that humans rank and satisfy needs in order of importance. He categorised human needs into five broad groups, developed in the form of a hierarchical pyramid, ranging from physiological needs at the base, and self-actualisation needs at the top of the pyramid. Once the basic physiological needs are satisfied, the needs of the next level take precedence and dominate motivation. The ascending nature of the model implies that we move in sequence from the base of the pyramid to the top in order to achieve our full potential, and this pattern of need satisfaction is the cause of motivation for the individual.

The fundamental tenets of the model are as follows:

- A satisfied need no longer motivates.
- Needs are hierarchical, which means that, in general, a person is driven by a higher-order need only after a primary need is satisfied.

---

[4]Maslow, A (1962). *Toward a Psychology of Being*. New York: Van Nostrand.

- The hierarchy reflects the priority of each need, which rises in importance up along the levels.

This idea establishes the position that once primary needs are satisfied, a higher-order need becomes the central preoccupation of a person, and the drive to satisfy this need motivates behaviour.

The term 'self-actualisation' refers to the motive to realise one's full potential, and to become everything that one is capable of becoming. The specific form that these needs take vary greatly from person to person; in one individual it may be expressed as the desire to become a mother, whereas in another, it could be the desire to become a painter. In essence, needs are both universal but unique to all individuals.[5]

Maslow stated that the hierarchy is not, in fact, rigidly fixed in a particular order; in general, people tend to follow the hierarchy but there are some exceptions to this behaviour. For instance, self-esteem may be more important to some people than love. Primary needs can be unsatisfied while a higher-order need such as esteem may indeed have been fulfilled; for instance, an employee may experience a lack of financial security in a job while at the same time experiencing high personal esteem from a manager recognising his good performance.[6]

The need hierarchy is useful for examining differences in motivation from one country to another. For example, in Greece and Japan, security needs may motivate employees more than self-actualisation needs. Likewise, belonging needs are especially important in Sweden, Norway and Denmark. Research has also found differences in the relative importance of different needs in Mexico, India, Peru, Canada, Thailand, Turkey and Puerto Rico.[7]

Role in the organisation today

Maslow's hierarchy of needs has become a referential model in the business environment in terms of understanding employee needs. It is useful for illustrating the fact that people are motivated by needs on several different levels (Figure 2.3).

---

[5]Maslow, A (1962). *Toward a Psychology of Being*. New York: Van Nostrand.
[6]Maslow, AH (1943). A theory of human motivation. *Psychological Review*, 50, 390–396.
[7]Adler, N (1997). *International Dimensions of Organizational Behavior*. Boston: PWS-Kent.

Challenging projects, opportunities for creativity, learning, growth.

Respect, recognition from others, prestige, status, personal esteem.

Acceptance, being part of a group, identification with a successful team.

Physical safety, economic security, freedom from threats, job security.

Physical survival needs: water, food, sleep...

SELF ACTUALIZATION

EGO (ESTEEM)

SOCIAL (BELONGING)

SAFETY / SECURITY

PHYSIOLOGICAL

Self-actualization needs are the hardest to satisfy in the workplace. Working towards self-actualization may be the ultimate motivation for most people.

Esteem needs in the workplace are met by job titles, office size, merit pay increases, awards, and other forms of recognition.

In the workplace, managers can help satisfy these needs by fostering a sense of group identity and interaction among employees.

Security needs in organizations can be satisfied by such things as job continuity (no layoffs), a grievance system, and an adequate insurance and retirement system.

Adequate wages, ventilation, and comfortable working environment are measures taken by companies to satisfy the most basic level of needs.

Adapted from Maslow (1943) by ESSEC ISIS

Figure 2.3   Role in the organisation today.

Although primary needs can be for the most part assured through the provision of a reasonable salary, a comfortable place to work, and through positive relations, the higher-order needs are somewhat subjective and less easy to provide for.[8] Today, the higher level needs of employees, represented by self-esteem and self-actualisation levels of the pyramid, are practiced through managerial approaches such as recognition, empowerment, opportunities for development, creativity, and so on.

Organisational Application

Understanding and providing opportunities for the attainment of both primary and higher-order needs is an important means for attracting, motivating and retaining employees. The following business application highlights the link between Maslow's hierarchy of needs and Siemens' approach to motivation.

---

[8]Vroom, VH and EL Deci (1970). *Management and Motivation*. Baltimore: Penguin Education.

Siemens provides the opportunity for employees to fulfil their higher-order needs. Feeling that a person's work is making a difference can improve his or her self-esteem. Recognition of an employee's achievements by the employer also helps to meet self-esteem needs of individuals. For example, Siemens runs schemes in which suggestions and projects for improvements are rewarded.

Self-actualisation is concerned with workers fulfilling their potential. Engineering work allows employees to do this by enabling them to get involved and take responsibility and ownership of their own jobs. Individuals in Siemens are encouraged to take the initiative to make improvements and changes. Original solutions and ideas are required to solve problems on a regular basis; this appeals to the higher-order needs of employees.

Siemens also offers engineering staff training and development opportunities to improve their competences. This links with self-actualisation as it helps engineers to improve their capabilities and progress up the career ladder. Training and development also helps individuals to meet the changing demands of the business' global markets.[9]

Lessons Learned

Maslow's hierarchy of needs classifies human needs into five categories. Divided into primary and higher-order needs, the lesson for managers is to begin with the provision of a safe, secure working environment and encourage positive interpersonal relationships, and then, to provide employees with opportunities for higher-order needs such as personal growth, advancement and self-fulfilment.[10]

2.3.2. *Existence-relatedness-growth needs*

Developed by Clayton P. Alderfer (1969).

Overview

Clayton P. Alderfer's need hierarchy model is composed of three core groups of needs: existence, relatedness and growth (ERG). Existence

---

[9]Motivation within a creative environment. The Times 100; http://www.thetimes100.co.uk/case-study–motivation-within-creative-environment–89-376-4.php.

[10]Maslow, AH (1943). A theory of human motivation. *Psychological Review*, 50, 390–396.

Figure 2.4   Existence-relatedness-growth model.

needs are concerned with needs that give us physical well-being: survival, physiological and safety needs. Relatedness needs are concerned with the need for social relationships. Growth needs refer to an intrinsic desire for personal development (Figure 2.4).[11]

Alderfer's model attempts to address the shortcomings of Maslow's need hierarchy; the chief difference is the assertion that several needs can exist simultaneously. Alderfer clearly demonstrates that more than one need may motivate an individual at the same time; primary needs do not have to be satisfied before a higher-level need emerges as a motivating influence. Despite being somewhat hierarchical in nature like Maslow's model, Alderfer's ERG model differs from that of Maslow by suggesting that people move around the hierarchy; for instance, an individual's growth need could be satisfied even though a relatedness need remains unsatisfied. Furthermore, the order of needs may differ from one person to another.

The Frustration-Regression Principle. Alderfer's model suggests that people can regress from a higher-order need to a primary need if they become frustrated in meeting this need; for example, due to lack of recognition for their work or a lack of opportunities for growth, an individual may 'regress' to the relatedness need by spending more time socialising with colleagues instead of focusing on work.[12]

---

[11] Alderfer, C (1969). An empirical test of a new theory of human needs. *Organizational Behavior and Human Performance*, 4(2), 142–175.
[12] Alderfer, C (1969). An empirical test of a new theory of human needs. *Organizational Behavior and Human Performance*, 4(2), 142–175.

Role in the organisation today

The message for managers is that policies and practices must be devised to help satisfy these three fundamental needs concurrently because such a step will result in fulfilled and motivated employees. Furthermore, the idea that motivation is driven by multiple needs and must be balanced by the organisation is important to prevent regression to lower-level needs and accordingly lower performance.

Organisational Application

Hitachi, a Japanese company based in California, is putting the existence-relatedness-growth model into action. Hitachi enjoys the benefits of retaining employees for a long period by ensuring the fulfilment of their essential needs and by recognising that an employee has multiple needs to be satisfied simultaneously.

Existence: Hitachi provides amply for the employee's 'existence' needs. A competitive salary and bonus programme allows team members to engage in a secure standard of living.

Relatedness: Hitachi addresses the 'relatedness' needs with the many committees that bring team members together from different departments. These committees include the community action committee, the employee events committee, the safety committee and the morale committee. Each committee has the goal of getting a group of individuals to work together, i.e., people that do not necessarily work together on a daily basis.

Growth: The tuition assistance programme allows team members to attend classes outside of work with the knowledge that the company will subsidise the cost of education, if the course relates to their position within the organisation. Additionally, team members are given the opportunity for growth, both personally and professionally, through the various seminars, conferences and expositions that team members are invited or, in some cases, required to attend.[13]

---

[13]Motivation at Hitachi Automotive Products; http://www.echeat.com/essay.php?t= 27240.

Lessons Learned

Alderfer's existence-relatedness-growth (ERG) model of needs introduces
the idea that there are three principal needs that can be of simultaneous
importance to the employee. The ERG theory is more adaptable to
the working environment than Maslow's model: the theory implies that
needs must be managed by the organisation to ensure that employees
continually have opportunities to satisfy needs in order for motivation
to be continually stimulated at work.

2.3.3. *Two Factors of Needs: Hygiene and Motivators*

Developed by Frederick Herzberg (1959).

Overview

Frederick Herzberg introduced a new concept to the study of motivation
by needs with the idea that different needs have different impacts on the
motivation of people at work. He distinguished between two types of needs:
hygiene factors, which cause dissatisfaction and demotivation if they are
unfulfilled, and motivator factors, which cause satisfaction, and can also
have a significantly positive impact on motivation. The combined effect
of both hygiene factors and motivators can help to satisfy all needs of
employees and stimulate motivation (Figure 2.5).

Herzberg asked his sample of blue-collar workers two questions:

  i. When did you feel satisfied in work?
 ii. When did you feel dissatisfied in work?

When he analysed the results of the survey, Herzberg found that the
factors contributing to satisfaction were not, in fact, the opposite of the
factors contributing to dissatisfaction. He found that 81% of the factors
contributing to job satisfaction were motivators, which led to growth and
development, and 69% of the factors contributing to job dissatisfaction were
hygiene factors, such as pay or interpersonal relations.

Hygiene factors refer to external environmental factors in work such as
salary, security, interpersonal relationships, physical working conditions and
HR practices, and these factors correspond to the primary needs for security,
safety, interpersonal relationships, and so on, as are found in the base levels
of Maslow's hierarchy. Motivator factors relate directly to the job itself

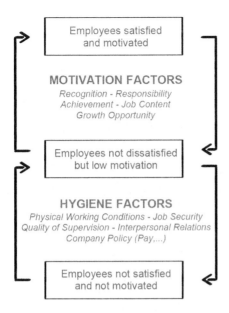

Adapted from Herzberg (1959) by ESSEC ISIS (2010)

Figure 2.5   Two factors of needs: Hygiene and motivators.

and correspond with the higher-order needs in Maslow's hierarchy. They refer to intrinsic factors of the job such as responsibilities, opportunities for promotion, autonomy, work challenge, task meaningfulness and interest.[14]

According to Herzberg, inadequate financial reward can demotivate employees, but nevertheless, money is a hygiene factor and beyond a certain level, it does not motivate the employee; in other words, it does not contribute to sustained motivation. According to Herzberg's two-factor theory, it is necessary to enrich and enlarge job content, and concurrently satisfy hygiene factors to a certain level, to ensure sustained motivation, employee satisfaction and performance.

Role in the organisation today

Herzberg provided managers with a new angle to understanding the motivation puzzle: the satisfaction of all needs does not generate the

---

[14]Amabile, TM (1993). Motivational synergy: Toward new conceptualizations of intrinsic and extrinsic motivation in the workplace. *Human Resource Management Review*, 3(3), 185–201.

same type of motivation. People will strive to achieve 'hygiene' needs because they are unhappy without them, but once satisfied, the effect soon wears off — satisfaction is temporary. But on the other hand, a person will not be positively or sustainably motivated unless intrinsic needs are also addressed. This relates to the idea that a satisfied need no longer motivates. Thus when the need for a certain level of hygiene needs is satisfied, it no longer drives motivation. However, because intrinsic needs, such as the need for esteem and professional development, are never absolutely satisfied, they continue to act as a source of motivation (Figure 2.6).

There is a dual lesson for organisations:

— Herzberg confirms that responding to the individual's primary needs is necessary to achieve satisfaction, while at the same time being an indispensable precondition for motivation. The organisation should

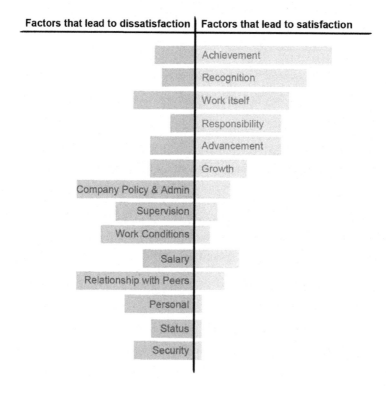

Source: Herzberg (1968)

Figure 2.6 Factors that lead to dissatisfaction compared to the factors that lead to satisfaction.

take care to ensure that employee needs for hygiene factors are met through the provision of safe, secure working environment and adequate compensation. As Figure 2.6 illustrates, factors such as company policy or relationships with peers can have a significant impact on dissatisfaction if unfulfilled.

— Herzberg emphasises the power of the intrinsic factors of motivation such as achievement, recognition, the work itself, responsibility and advancement as essential drivers of motivation.[15]

Organisational Application

A report by the European Agency for Safety and Health at Work concluded that a healthy work environment can have 'a positive impact not only on safety and health performance but also on company productivity' and that a poor environment 'can lead to a competitive disadvantage impairing the firm's status among stakeholders'. For example, a study in the year 2000 of nearly 4,000 employees at the Polaroid Corporation documented a reduction in absenteeism through the use of enhanced ventilation using outdoor air. In 2003, a field simulation study was conducted by the Lighting Research Center at Rensselaer Polytechnic Institute and National Research Council of Canada that indicated a causal relationship between lighting quality and worker satisfaction and motivation.[16]

Lessons Learned

Human needs in the workplace fall into two categories: hygiene factors, which are necessary to maintain employee satisfaction and are indispensable for creating an environment that is propitious to motivation; and motivator factors, which refer to opportunities for growth, esteem and self-actualisation. The theory demonstrates the decisive role that both hygiene factors and the satisfaction of psychological needs for growth and self-actualisation play in the motivation of employees.

[15]Herzberg, F, B Mausner and RD Peterson (1957). *Job Attitudes: Review of Research and Options.* Pittsburgh, PA: Psychological Service of Pittsburgh.

[16]Wiedenkeller, K (2010). SVP, Human resources, AMC entertainment in 'Some like it hot? Work environments impact productivity', *Film Journal International*, 4 May 2010; http://www.filmjournal.com/filmjournal/content_display/columns-and-blogs/the-people-factor/e3i7b2c50df9c8f86ff8be25b86bc20bd72.

2.4. Intrinsic Motivation by Higher-Order Needs

The theories in the following section focus on the higher levels of Maslow's hierarchy, which relate to higher-order or psychological needs. Higher-order needs create intrinsic motivation at work.[17]

Intrinsic motivation at work involves employees doing an activity because they find it interesting and derive spontaneous satisfaction from the activity itself. Individuals are intrinsically motivated when they seek enjoyment, satisfaction of curiosity, self-expression, or personal challenge at work. The rewards, such as feelings of accomplishment, feelings of achievement, and feeling that one is using and developing one's skills and abilities, are internally mediated and satisfy higher-order needs such as esteem and self-actualisation.[18]

Extrinsic motivation at work entails an instrumentality between the activity and consequences that are separate to the task itself, such as tangible, contingent or verbal rewards. Satisfaction does not come from the activity itself but rather from the extrinsic consequences to which the activity leads. Contingent rewards are defined as rewards that are tied to the task or to a level of performance. Extrinsic motivators include anything from an outside source that is intended to influence the initiation or the performance of the work: promised reward, praise, critical feedback, deadlines, surveillance, or specifications on the work itself.

The two motivational types so often co-occur in work situations: one can be intrinsically motivated by the interest in the task and at the same time extrinsically motivated to complete a task in time for a deadline. Managers need to be innovative in the proposition of new motivation solutions based on enhancing interest in the activity itself as well as relying on extrinsic motivation factors.[19]

The following theories explore the concept of intrinsic motivation and are driven by higher-order needs. Deci and Ryan (1985), Herzberg (1969) and Hackman and Oldman (1980) have developed models relating to this concept. Deci and Ryan introduced the idea that intrinsic motivation is caused by the innate needs to feel competent, self-determined, and the

---

[17]Vroom, VH and EL Deci (1970). *Management and Motivation*. Baltimore: Penguin Education.
[18]Vroom, VH and EL Deci (1970). *Management and Motivation*. Baltimore: Penguin Education.
[19]Hennessey, BA and TM Amabile (1998). Reward, intrinsic motivation, and creativity. *American Psychologist*, 53(6), 674–675.

need for relatedness. Herzberg views intrinsic and extrinsic motivation as combining additively to produce motivation resulting from a combination of external and internal job characteristics. Hackman and Oldman argue that there are characteristics which jobs must possess in order to stimulate higher-order needs.[20]

2.4.1. Self-Determination

Developed by Edward L. Deci and Richard M. Ryan (1971).

Overview

To be self-determining means an employee experiences a sense of choice in initiating and regulating his or her actions. It suggests that people have a *need* to feel autonomous and competent. The concept of self-determination is similar in meaning to Maslow's higher-order need for self-actualisation: the notion that the organisational culture allows an employee the opportunity or freedom to reach his or her full potential.[21]

According to Deci and Ryan, each individual develops two needs in tandem: the need to feel competent and the need for self-determination. The need for competence refers to the necessity to develop one's abilities and to efficiently interact with the working environment. The need for self-determination refers to the need to feel capable of choosing, to feel empowered, and to be responsible for one's own behaviour as much as possible.[22]

According to Deci and Ryan, intrinsic motivation is based chiefly on the innate human needs for competence and self-determination; relatedness also plays a role to a lesser extent. The needs for competence and self-determination energises behaviours for which the primary rewards are the experiences of achievement and autonomy. Intrinsic needs differ from primary need drives in that they are not based on physiological drives. Like drives, however, intrinsic needs are innate to humans and function as an important energiser of behaviour. The intrinsic needs for competence and self-determination motivate a continual process of seeking to conquer challenges. A challenge may be defined as something that

---

[20]Vroom, VH and EL Deci (1970). *Management and Motivation*. Baltimore: Penguin Education.

[21]Deci, EL and RM Ryan (1985). *Intrinsic Motivation and Self-Determination in Human Behavior*. New York: Plenum Press.

[22]Deci, EL and RM Ryan (1985). *Intrinsic Motivation and Self-Determination in Human Behavior*. New York: Plenum Press.

requires extending one's abilities and trying new things. When people are intrinsically motivated, they experience interest and enjoyment; they feel competent and self-determining.[23]

In the work environment, the interaction between the manager and the subordinate can be interpreted by the employee in two ways that affect self-determination: as *informational* or *controlling*. Rewards, deadlines, or positive feedback are all positive contributors to an employee's self-determination if they are understood by the employee to be informational and not controlling, depending on the style of management. Threats of punishment, surveillance and evaluations tend to be experienced as controlling, and thus negatively affecting the employee's sense of choice, self-esteem, intrinsic motivation and perceived competence.[24]

Promoting self-determination in the workplace involves three main factors: support for autonomy (allowing choice); non-controlling positive feedback and acknowledging and accepting the employee's perspective.

Role in the organisation today

The theory of self-determination is increasingly important in terms of creating an environment that enables a certain level of autonomy and empowerment. Self-determination has been linked to enhanced creativity, self-esteem, conceptual learning and general well-being and is supported by participation of the employee in decision making, support for individual initiative and open communications. Intrinsic motivation is associated with increased interest in the task, increased engagement and higher performance due to the motivation to feel competent.[25]

A combination of both intrinsic and extrinsic motivational practices may have an additive and positive effect on motivation.[26] It has been found that when intrinsic motivation is high, tangible extrinsic rewards can positively contribute to overall motivation.[27] Additionally, when the

---

[23]Deci, EL and RM Ryan (1985). *Intrinsic Motivation and Self-Determination in Human Behavior*. New York: Plenum Press.

[24]Deci, EL *et al.* (1989). Self-determination in a work organization. *Journal of Applied Psychology*, 74(4), 580–590.

[25]Deci, EL *et al.* (1989). Self-determination in a work organization. *Journal of Applied Psychology*, 74(4), 580–590.

[26]Porter, LW and EE Lawlor (1968). *Managerial Attitudes and Performance*. Homewood, IL: Irwin-Dorsey.

[27]Deci, EL, R Koestner and RM Ryan (1999). A meta-analytic review of experiments examining the effects of extrinsic rewards on intrinsic motivation. *Psychological Bulletin*, 125, 627–668.

interpersonal work environment is supportive rather than pressurising, tangible rewards (even when they are contingent on high-performance) can be positive.[28] Recognition, when it provides people with positive information about their self-competence, supports intrinsic motivation.

Organisational Application

Semco SA (Semco), a Brazilian manufacturing company, saw its revenues grow from $32 million in 1990 to $212 million in 2003. Between 1982 and 1998, Semco's productivity increased nearly seven-fold and profits rose five-fold. Semco was also one of the most sought-after Brazilian companies in terms of employment. Turnover among its 3,000 employees was about 1% during the period 1994 to 2004. Repeat customers accounted for around 80% of Semco's 2003 annual revenues.

The culture at Semco was unique in the sense that there were no hierarchical, power-packed job titles; employees including top managers themselves did the photocopying, sent faxes, typed letters and made and received phone calls. There were no executive dining rooms, and parking was strictly first-come, first-served. Organisational profits were shared with the employees and the salaries were set by the employees themselves. Behind this organisation was Ricardo Semler, the CEO of the company, who referred to himself as the Chief Enzyme Officer.

Semler started out with a functional organisational structure at Semco but decided to divide the company into small business units to remove hierarchy and increase team collaboration and empowerment. The organisation was bound together by the three interdependent core values: employee participation, profit sharing and free flow of information. These three values stemmed from the belief that participation in design and implementation of work procedures would give employees control over their work; profit-sharing would bring a sense of ownership; and the availability of information would help the employees improve their work practices continuously or when needed.[29]

---

[28]Ryan, RM, V Mims and R Koestner (1983). Relation of reward contingency and interpersonal context to intrinsic motivation: A review and test using cognitive evaluation theory. *Journal of Personality and Social Psychology*, 45, 736–750.

[29]Semco: A Maverick Organization (2004); http://www.icmrindia.org/casestudies/catalogue/Human%20Resource%20and%20Organization%20Behavior/HROB060.htm.

Lessons Learned

Self-determination occurs when the employee experiences choice in his or her actions at work; he does not feel overly controlled by the organisation and has the freedom to realise objectives in an autonomous way. It is important to allow employees a certain degree of autonomy to enable them to be self-determined and competent, two of the most important factors contributing to intrinsic motivation.

2.4.2. Job Enrichment

Developed by Frederick Herzberg (1969).

Overview

Following on from Herzberg's two-factor theory, we will take a closer look at the notion of 'motivators', which have been developed by Herzberg in the concept of job enrichment. Motivators are the factors that meet the human need for psychological growth (achievement, recognition, responsibility, advancement); these are factors, according to Herzberg, that are concerned with an increase in the satisfaction of higher-order needs — job content or the work itself. In other words, the job itself becomes the prime vehicle of all individual development.[30]

Herzberg's theory of job enrichment entails 'enriching' people's jobs by building in greater scope for personal achievement, recognition, more challenging and responsible work and more opportunity for individual advancement and growth; it aims to improve task efficiency and job satisfaction.[31] Herzberg argues that job enrichment, which is based on the notion that individual growth is key to organisational health, is the approach that most often results in happier employees and higher productivity.[32] He felt that one of the primary causes of job dissatisfaction is that most jobs have been robbed of meaning in the name of efficiency.[33]

---

[30] Herzberg, F (1979). The wise old turk. *Harvard Business Review*, 52, 70–81.
[31] William PJ, KB Robertson and F Herzberg (1969). Job enrichment pays off. *Harvard Business Review*, 47(2), 61–78.
[32] Herzberg, F (1979). The wise old turk. *Harvard Business Review*, 52, 70–81.
[33] Herzberg, F (1979). The wise old turk. *Harvard Business Review*, 52, 70–81.

He felt that greater opportunities for motivation are to be found in the interest and meaningfulness of the job itself, opportunities for advancement and recognition for the task.

Herzberg's eight building blocks of a good job are as follows:

- *Direct feedback*: Knowing the results of one's behaviour is essential to efficient learning and performance and provides the individual with the information to enable improvement or recognition of performance.
- *A client relationship*: Connecting tasks with a beneficiary provides higher task meaningfulness; this need not necessarily be the client *per se*, but a co-worker or another beneficiary of the task.
- *New learning*: The importance of purposeful learning to enable psychological growth.
- *Self-scheduling*: The opportunity for each person to schedule his own work; the person completing the task is in the best position to estimate the length of time required to complete the task; allowing personal responsibility over task scheduling results in an increased sense of autonomy.
- *Unique expertise*: Task homogenisation and assembly-line operations incite boredom and decrease motivation over time; there is a need to incorporate an element of uniqueness in the job content to allow the individual time for creativity or to perform other tasks of personal interest.
- *Control over resources*: Greater autonomy in purchases leads to greater responsibility in terms of expenditure.
- *Direct communications authority*: Eliminating barriers to communication and allowing direct vertical communication leads to greater efficiency and a greater sense of responsibility.
- *Personal accountability*: Too many controls divide responsibility until it gets lost and nobody is accountable; accountability gives an individual more pride in his or her work and entails an 'ownership of errors'.

Herzberg notes the importance of assessing the individual's abilities, needs and potentials in order to ascertain to what degree the job enrichment must occur: employees are not homogeneous in terms of needs and capabilities.[34]

---

[34]William PJ, KB Robertson and F Herzberg (1969). Job enrichment pays off. *Harvard Business Review*, 47(2), 61–78.

Role in the organisation today

Many of the concepts of job enrichment are indeed relevant in today's organisation. The global workforce is no longer satisfied with homogeneous tasks and assembly-line repetition. Moreover, the importance of individual creativity and thinking 'outside the box' is key to corporate competitiveness and the development of innovative solutions, a practice that can only flourish in organisations which encourage free-thinking, employee empowerment and variety of tasks.[35] Job enrichment also underlines the importance of training to ensure employees retain the ability to do their job properly, and the importance of an appraisal system that reinforces growth and achievement (Figure 2.7).

The introduction of job enrichment should be preceded by consultation with the employee as individual employees tend to have different perspectives on what constitutes an interesting job.[36] Feedback and continual evaluation are also important for ensuring effective implementation.[37]

Adapted from Herzberg (1974) by ESSEC ISIS (2010)

Figure 2.7   Job enrichment.

---

[35]Amabile, T (1998). How to kill creativity. *Harvard Business Review*, September–October, 77–87.

[36]William, PJ, KB Robertson and F Herzberg (1969). Job enrichment pays off. *Harvard Business Review*, 47(2); 61–78.

[37]Minor, JB (2005). *Essential Theories of Motivation and Leadership.* New York: M.E. Sharpe.

Organisational Application

Car manufacturing plants have traditionally been associated with negative worker morale due to the repetitive production line process. The traditional 'Fordist' assembly line approach has been associated with two major problems: (1) musculoskeletal disorders caused by repetitive work with a very short cycle time and, (2) low levels of employee autonomy and responsibility make the work unattractive, resulting in low employee morale.

Volvo introduced a strategy of job enrichment to its factories in the 1990s to improve worker morality and motivation, and to reduce turnover and absenteeism. The management decided to experiment with five job enrichment measures — job rotation, management–employee councils, small work groups, change implementation, and employee-oriented facilities — at its manufacturing facilities. Developing staff competence was deemed vital by Volvo to build quality cars as well as to achieve the organisational objectives of improving productivity, flexibility and efficiency.[38]

Lessons Learned

Herzberg's theory of job enrichment is an attempt to provide for employee higher-order needs for growth, esteem and self-actualisation through the job content. In other words, the job itself becomes the prime vehicle of all individual development and motivation and is an important method for increasing intrinsic motivation in work today.

2.4.3. *Job Characteristics*

Developed by Richard Hackman and Greg Oldham (1980).

Overview

Job content is believed to be a critical determinant of whether employees believe that good performance on the job leads to feelings of

---

[38]Volvo's HR Practices: Job enrichment (2004); http://www.icmrindia.org/casestudies/catalogue/Human%20Resource%20and%20Organization%20Behavior/Volvo%20HR%20Practices-Job%20Enrichment-Human%20Resource%20Management-Case%20Studies.htm.

Valuing People to Create Value

accomplishment, growth and self-esteem; these factors determine whether a job is intrinsically motivating. Hackman and Oldham state that there are three main characteristics that jobs must possess if they are to stimulate higher-order needs and to create conditions so that performance will lead to intrinsic rewards. The first is that the individual must receive meaningful feedback about his performance. The second is that the job must be perceived by the individual as requiring the use of his abilities or skills in order for him to perform the job effectively; valuing an employee's skills can lead to feelings of accomplishment and growth. Finally, the individual must feel that he has a high degree of self-control over setting his or her own goals and deciding how he or she will achieve these goals (Figure 2.8).[39]

Hackman and Oldham argue that job enlargement is essential for optimal intrinsic motivation. There are two main types of job enlargement: horizontal and vertical job enlargement. They posit that both are necessary for optimal intrinsic motivation. Horizontal job enlargement refers to the number and variety of operations that an individual performs on the job; for instance, for an employee working on a production line, a system of job rotation can prevent task boredom and stimulate interest in the job. Vertical job enlargement refers to the degree to which the employee controls

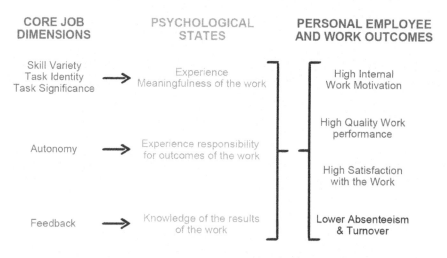

Adapted from Hackman & Oldham by ESSEC ISIS (2010)

Figure 2.8   Intrinsic motivation: Job characteristics.

---

[39]Vroom, VH and EL Deci (1970). *Management and Motivation*. Baltimore: Penguin Education.

the planning and execution of the job and participates in decision-making; for instance, many companies have increased the interaction with employees to incorporate their opinions in terms of decision-making.[40]

Role in the organisation today

In contemporary working environments, job content represents an integral tool for optimising motivation. Companies that recognise the necessity of enriching tasks will reap the rewards of higher employee motivation. The French postal service, La Poste, uses a process of task versatility whereby employees change tasks every three hours to prevent tedium and maintain motivation.

Organisational designs that permit greater participation in decision-making and greater flexibility in doing one's job have been found to be positively associated with employee satisfaction, quality of work life and organisational effectiveness.[41] Many car manufacturing plants, such as Toyota, Ferrari and Volvo, have implemented some form of job enrichment. The process is found to result in higher quality production, and lower rates of absenteeism; yet, it may pose a challenge in terms of implementation costs and maintaining competitiveness.[42]

Organisational Application

IBM implemented a process of job enrichment in the 1940s; there was a particular demand for increased quality in machining and assembly work and for this reason job enrichment represented a favourable practice to improve the product quality. Many opportunities for the education of the employees were introduced and attendance records increased markedly with the introduction of job enlargement.[43]

---

[40]Vroom, VH and EL Deci (1970). *Management and Motivation*. Baltimore: Penguin Education.

[41]Hackman, JR and EE Lawlor (1971). Employee reactions to job characteristics. *Journal of Applied Psychology*, 55, 259–286.

[42]Jang, JS, SC Rim and SC Park (2006). Reforming a conventional vehicle assembly plant for job enrichment. *International Journal of Production Research*, 44(4), 703–713.

[43]Walker, C (1949). The problem of a repetitive job, *Harvard Business Review*, from a paper given by James C. Worth at the Fifth Annual Meeting of the American Sociological Society, New York City, December 29 1949.

Lessons Learned

Hackman and Oldham argue that when jobs are structured in a way that intrinsic rewards result from performance, then the job itself can be a very effective motivator. If job content is to be a source of motivation, the job must allow for meaningful feedback, it must test the individual's valued abilities and allow a high level of self-control by the employee. For this to occur, jobs must be enlarged horizontally (increased variety of tasks) and vertically (increased responsibility or autonomy).

2.5. Summary

2.5.1. *Summary of Need-Motivation Models*

The first three need motivation models look at the entire range of human needs and how they motivate individuals to work; ranging from the primary (physiological) human needs such as the need for food or shelter, to the higher-order (psychological) needs such as the need for growth, esteem or self-determination. Each model presents a different perspective on the range of human needs that contribute to motivation at work.

Motivation Theory	Summary	Role in Motivation at Work
Maslow, 1943: Hierarchy of Needs	A hierarchic model of human needs: from primary needs (food, shelter...) at the base of the pyramid, to high-order needs (esteem, self-actualisation...) at the top levels. Humans are driven to satisfy needs in order of importance.	Employee needs lie at the root of motivated behaviour; motivation at work can be partly explained by the drive to satisfy needs. The organisation must provide the means to satisfy human needs in order to motivate employees to perform their job.
Alderfer, 1969: Existence Relatedness Growth (ERG) Theory	Alderfer's existence-relatedness-growth (ERG) model is based on Maslow's needs model. He introduced the idea that three main needs can be of simultaneous importance to the individual.	The ERG theory is more adaptable to the working environment: the theory implies that three fundamental needs must be managed by the organisation to ensure that employees continually have opportunities to satisfy needs, and thus to be motivated at work.

(Continued)

(*Continued*)

Motivation Theory	Summary	Role in Motivation at Work
Herzberg, 1959: Two-factor Theory: Motivation and hygiene factors	Human needs in the workplace fall into two categories: hygiene factors, which are necessary to prevent employee dissatisfaction, and motivation factors such as opportunities for growth, esteem and self-actualisation, which lead to motivation when combined with adequate hygiene factors.	This theory highlights the importance of a good working environment and opportunities for intrinsic motivation in the form of higher-order needs. The combination of both adequate environmental factors and opportunities for satisfying psychological needs are key to motivating employees.

2.5.2. *Summary of Higher-Order Need-Motivation Models*

The theories in higher-order need motivation focus on the higher levels of Maslow's hierarchy, the levels of higher-order or psychological needs. These higher-order needs are concerned with the psychological needs at the higher levels of Maslow's hierarchy of needs. The higher-order needs are responsible for intrinsic motivation at work.

Motivation Theory	Summary	Role in Motivation at Work
Deci and Ryan, 1971: Self-determination	Self-determination occurs when the employee experiences choice in his actions at work; he or she does not feel overly controlled by the organisation and has the freedom to realise objectives in an autonomous way.	It is important to allow employees a certain degree of autonomy to enable them to be self-determined and competent, two of the most important factors in intrinsic motivation. Intrinsic motivation means that the employee experiences enjoyment and interest in the task, through the satisfaction of higher-order needs for competence and self-determination.
Herzberg, 1968: Job enrichment	Herzberg's theory of job enrichment aims to provide for employee higher-order needs for growth, esteem and self-actualisation through the job content.	Herzberg's job enrichment model promotes the benefits of adapting jobs to be more interesting, challenging, and providing opportunities for advancement in order to create long-term motivation.

(*Continued*)

(*Continued*)

Motivation Theory	Summary	Role in Motivation at Work
Oldham and Hackman, 1971: Job characteristics theory	Human needs in the workplace fall into two categories: hygiene factors, which are necessary to maintain employee satisfaction, and motivator factors, which refer to opportunities for growth, esteem and self-actualisation.	This theory recognises the importance of maintaining a working environment that is propitious to employee satisfaction; opportunities for satisfying psychological needs are crucial for motivating employees.

Chapter 3

THE PROCESSES OF MOTIVATION AT WORK

The processes of motivation at work focus on the cognitive processes that translate the building blocks (needs) into action. People evaluate situations, tasks and behaviours, and make calculations or choices on where to direct their effort in work. The cognitive processes of expectancy, achievement, attribution, reinforcement, learning, and rewards play a key role in guiding motivated behaviour at the workplace.

This chapter explores the cognitive processes that translate needs into action. We understand from Chapter 2 ('The Building Blocks of Motivation') that behaviour at work is guided by the satisfaction of needs or goals.[1] These needs function as internal motives or impulses that stimulate a person's effort at work; they form the basis of why we go to work, the efforts we exert to perform a task, and the reason we seek the satisfaction of different needs from day to day or over the course of our working lives.[2] But what processes guide the choices people make about which needs to satisfy?

In order to understand *how* exactly these needs and motives actually drive behaviour in the workplace, we must look at the *cognitive thought processes* that cause needs to be translated into a chosen path of action. People evaluate situations, tasks, and behaviours and make calculations

---

[1]Vroom, VH and EL Deci (1970). *Management and Motivation.* Baltimore: Penguin Education.

[2]Robbins, SP and DA DeCenzo (2008). *Fundamentals of Management: Essential Concepts and Applications.* New Jersey: Pearson Prentice Hall.

or choices on where to direct their effort in work.[3] In this chapter, we examine the ability of the individual to discriminate between tasks and exert different levels of effort based on their individual evaluation of their ability to perform a task, the perceived likelihood of task success, and the value that they place on the successful completion of the task.[4] In other words, this chapter explores how well an individual expects to perform a task and what reward he or she can expect from completing the task well.

The 'processes' of motivation focus on how the expectancy of performance outcomes and rewards drive performance at work; how learning from past experience guides behaviour; and how individual need for achievement drives performance. An individual calculates choices based on his or her personal expectation of the outcome of his or her effort. This expectation may be formed based either on past experiences that provide a yardstick for the outcome of effort, or on a person's estimation of the outcome of the effort. This means that the outcome of a task functions as a goal or incentive for the individual: it may be the achievement of the task itself, or may correspond to the satisfaction of a need through rewards or recognition.[5]

3.1.   Overview of the Chapter

The chapter is divided into two sections that focus on two different cognitive concepts: expectancy and learning.

We first look at the model of expectancy theory, which is the chief model that explains the cognitive process associated with rewards and the role that a person's expectancy of an outcome plays in motivating behaviour. Subsequently we look at the expectancy process that relates to achievement motivation, the process by which expectancy of task success will lead high achievers to perform a task. The third model of expectancy looks at how attributions (explanations) of prior task success or failure influence an individual's expectancy for task success in future behaviour, and accordingly, the implication on motivation.

The second section looks at the process of learning through which people 'learn' behaviours in the organisation. This occurs through two processes: reinforcement and social learning. Reinforcement is the process by which individuals learn, through the consequences associated with

---

[3]Tolman, EC (1932). *Purposive Behaviour in Animals*. New York: Appleton-Century-Crofts.
[4]Vroom, V (1964). *Work and Motivation*. New York: John Wiley and Sons.
[5]Vroom, V (1964). *Work and Motivation*. New York: John Wiley and Sons.

past behaviour, to follow certain patterns of behaviour. Social learning looks at the learning that takes place through observations of others in the organisation. Both theories underline the importance of the role of consequences on behaviour.

3.1.1. *Glossary of Key Definitions for 'The Processes of Motivation at Work'*

Expectancy: The term 'expectancy' refers to the idea that people form expectations about the outcomes of an event and make decisions on how to direct their effort to complete a task. They form an expectation that corresponds to their perceived ability to complete a task successfully, and they also form an expectation of the outcomes of the task completion.

Valence: The term valence refers to the attractiveness or value of a particular goal or outcome. A goal or outcome that corresponds with the satisfaction of a primary or higher-order need holds an incentive value for the individual.

Instrumentality: This is the link between performance and reward and lies in the belief that one's performance will be rewarded. The reward may be the achievement of the task, or an extrinsic reward such as a bonus.

Achievement: Intense, prolonged, and repeated efforts to accomplish something difficult and to work with singularity of purpose towards a high and distant goal. To have the determination to win.

Reinforcement: Desirable behaviours can be encouraged by linking those behaviours with positive consequences, and undesirable behaviours can be discouraged by linking them with negative consequences.

3.2. Motivation by Expectancy

The idea of motivation by expectancy is underpinned by the ancient Greek concept of hedonism, the central idea of which is the human pursuit of pleasure and avoidance of pain. Individuals make a calculation based on the optimisation of 'pleasure' and the minimisation of 'pain'; in other words, the individual's efforts are directed towards outcomes that are valued by the individual as pleasurable.[6]

---

[6]Pinder, C (1998). *Work Motivation in Organizational Behavior*. Upper Saddle River, NJ: Prentice Hall.

Cognitive theories of motivating behaviour can be traced back to the pioneering work of Tolman and Lewin who established the idea that we are essentially 'purposeful' beings and the establishment of goals or purposes guides our behaviour towards the accomplishment of these goals. This idea of purposiveness or directing behaviour towards a valued goal or outcome is explained by expectancy theory, and represents a central process of motivation at work.[7]

Thus, motivation by expectancy presents the concept that people make choices regarding their behaviour at work based on the expectancy that performance will lead to certain valued outcomes or goals. There are two levels of outcomes that influence choice: first level outcomes relate to the actual performance or completion of the task; second level outcomes refer to the rewards that accompany task success such as a bonus, recognition from the supervisor, the feeling of achievement, and so on.

3.2.1. *Motivation by Expectancy: Values and Rewards*

Developed by Victor Vroom (1964); and Edward E. Lawler and Lyman W. Porter (1968).

Overview

Expectancy theory states that people are rational decision makers who think about their actions and act in ways that satisfy their needs and help them reach their goals. Expectancy theory views people as proactive, future-oriented and motivated to behave in ways that they believe will lead to valued rewards.[8]

In work situations, people are motivated by the belief that they can expect to achieve certain desired rewards by working hard to attain them. The fundamental basis of expectancy theory proposes that human efforts are a function of the attractiveness of certain outcomes and the individual's estimation that these desired outcomes can be attained, i.e. people tend to prefer certain goals or outcomes over others. Workers rationally evaluate various work behaviours and then choose those that they will believe will

---

[7]Tolman, EC (1932). *Purposive Behaviour in Animals.* New York: Appleton-Century-Crofts; Lewin, K (1938). *The Conceptual Representation and the Measurement of Psychological Forces.* Durham, NC: Duke University Press.

[8]Lawler, EE and CG Worley (2006). Winning support for organizational change: Designing employee reward systems that keep on working. *Ivey Business Journal,* March/April, 1–5.

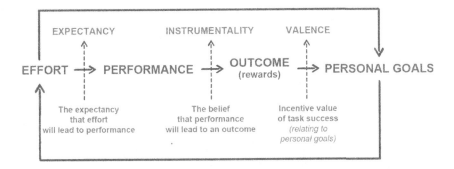

Adapted from Porter and Lawler (1968) by ESSEC ISIS (2010)

Figure 3.1 Expectancy value theory.

lead to the work-related rewards which they value the most. An individual's actions aim to optimise expected valence (or value) of the outcome and this directs their choice among alternative work-related outcomes.[9]

The important lesson for organisations is to understand exactly what people value as rewards, and aligning these rewards with employee and organisational goals or values.

Expectancy theory functions on three linked variables: Expectancy, instrumentality, and valence (Figure 3.1).

Expectancy: This is the perceived link between effort and performance: the belief that one's effort will result in performance. Expectancy is based on the individual's evaluation that exerting a given amount of effort will lead to performance.[10]

Organisational Application

Expectancy in a Factory Setting

An employee operating a faulty piece of equipment may have a low expectancy that his efforts will lead to a high level of performance. In these conditions, it would be unlikely that the employee would continue to exert the same level of effort when the performance outcome is low relative to the effort exerted.

---

[9]Ferris, KR (1977). A test of the expectancy theory of motivation in an accounting environment. *The Accounting Review*, 52(3), 605–615.
[10]Vroom, V (1964). *Work and Motivation*. New York: John Wiley and Sons; Porter, LW and EE Lawler (1968). *Managerial Attitudes and Performance*. Homewood, IL: Irwin.

Instrumentality: This is the link between performance and reward: the belief that one's performance will be rewarded. In the work context, a large part of working more effectively involves ensuring that efforts will pay off or be rewarded in some way; this may take the form of tangible rewards or psychological rewards. Many companies have developed pay systems that explicitly link desired performance to rewards.[11]

Organisational Application

Instrumentality in IBM

IBM decided to implement a pay plan to improve sales performance and client satisfaction. Employee pay is now linked to two factors that are deemed essential to the company's success — profitability and customer satisfaction. Instead of receiving commission on the amount of the sale, as is the norm in most sales companies, 60% of commission received by employees is linked to the IBM's *profit* on the sale. Therefore, the more the company makes, the more the sales reps make. To ensure employees do not only push high-profit items that are not necessarily what the customer needs, the remaining 40% of commissions are based on customer satisfaction. This linked organisational goals to employee goals proved to be successful as IBM succeeded in reversing an unprofitable trend.[12]

Valence: Valence refers to the perceived attractiveness or value of the expected rewards.[13] If a reward is not valued by the employee, the motivation to perform and attain such a reward is reduced. It is important to put in place a two-way communication system whereby employees can express which rewards they value, and to ensure that they are aware of the link between these rewards and performance. For operational effectiveness, the rewards need to be both clearly communicated to employees and they need to be of a perceived value. Rewards are not equally desirable to everyone. For example, a bonus given to a multimillionaire CEO would have to be much higher than a bonus for a minimum-wage employee in order for the value to be felt.

---

[11]Vroom, V (1964). *Work and Motivation.* New York: John Wiley and Sons; Porter, LW and EE Lawler (1968). *Managerial Attitudes and Performance.* Homewood, IL: Irwin.
[12]Walker, C (1949). *The Problem of a Repetitive Job.* Harvard Business Review, from a paper given by James C Worth at the Fifth Annual Meeting of the American Sociological Society, New York City, December 29.
[13]Vroom, V (1964). *Work and Motivation.* New York: John Wiley and Sons; Porter, LW and EE Lawler (1968). *Managerial Attitudes and Performance.* Homewood, IL: Irwin.

Organisational Application

Valence of Rewards

The global workforce of today is characterised by a high level of diversity and it would be a mistake to assume that employees are equally attracted to the same rewards. Increasingly, companies are introducing 'cafeteria-style benefit plans' through which employees can select their fringe benefits from a menu of available alternatives.

Role in the organisation today

Motivation by expectancy, values and rewards has demonstrated its widespread applicability and effectiveness in motivating individuals at work. Organisations need reward systems that motivate and reward performance, and encourage the development of individual and organisational capabilities and competencies.[14]

An important consideration of motivation by expectancy is the notion of perception or subjectivity: it is the individual beliefs about expectancy, instrumentality and valence that affect the motivational forces. The expectations of the link between effort and performance, as well as the valuation of the reward, are both subjective valuations from the employee. For this reason, and to avoid ambiguity, a clear system for communicating information about pay and benefits is essential to ensuring that the systems in place have an effect on performance.

Organisational Application

Rewards Strategy at Heinz UK and Ireland

The UK and Ireland division of Heinz has implemented a strategy to change the way its managers were rewarded. This involved aligning the company's goals more closely with its distribution of bonuses. Values such as achievement, accountability, integrity and urgency were established to underpin the firm's new reward mechanism, as well as to encourage desired behaviours in staff. 'One of the things we realised fairly early on was that, within Heinz, we were rewarding people for effort, and

---

[14]Lawler, EE and CG Worley (2006). Winning support for organizational change: Designing employee reward systems that keep on working. *Ivey Business Journal*, March/April, 1–5.

were not rewarding and encouraging a focus on results. We were trying to change that balance to ensure effort was always important and people were giving 100%. Even if people are giving discretionary effort, if you are not driving the results coming out of it, that is only half the battle,' says Nigel Perry, HR director for Heinz UK.

The UK and Ireland division is also carrying forward a number of initiatives to increase the spending power of frontline employees. It has revamped its reward offering by launching a voluntary benefits scheme to its 3,500 employees. Through the scheme, staff receive a discount card that they can use at a variety of retailers to buy household essentials, petrol and groceries. The scheme also gives members access to an online travel agency through which they can get discounts on flights and holidays.[15]

Lessons Learned

People will engage in motivated behaviour if they value the expected rewards, believe their efforts will lead to performance and understand that their performance will result in the desired rewards. Under the right combinations of expectancy, valences and outcomes, people will be highly motivated. The organisation should be familiar with the differences in employee values in rewards through evaluations and provide feedback to communicate on desirable performance.

3.2.2. *Motivation by Expectancy: Achievement*

Developed by Henry Murray (1938); and J. W. Atkinson (1964).

Overview

Achievement motivation refers to the concept of being motivated *to achieve*, which arises from an acquired (learned) need for achievement. A person with a high need for achievement has a strong motivation to perform tasks well (high standard of accomplishment), the desire to undertake new and challenging tasks (mastery) and the drive to surpass the performance of others (competitiveness).[16]

---

[15]Sullivan, N (2009). Full of Beans, *Employee Benefits*, April.
[16]Helmreich, RL and JT Spence (1978). The work and family orientation questionnaire: An objective instrument to assess components of achievement motivation and attitudes toward family and career. JSAS *Catalog of Selected Documents in Psychology*, 8, 35.

The term 'achievement' was first used by Henry Murray in 1938 and defined as '*intense, prolonged and repeated efforts to accomplish something difficult. To work with singularity of purpose towards a high and distant goal. To have the determination to win*'.[17]

Motivation for achievement propels the individual to seek success and to avoid failure. Individuals differ in the extent to which motives for success are stronger than motives to avoid failure. Individuals classified as oriented towards achievement or success, called high achievers, prefer and perform best on tasks of intermediate difficulty and persist longer at the task in the face of failure than persons classified as failure-oriented.[18]

Achievement motivation is a cognitive process calculated by the individual based on an assessment of expectancy of task success. Individuals motivated by achievement make choices in the type and level of perseverance of a task based on individual expectation of task success, and the perceived value of task success.[19]

Three variables — motive, expectancy and incentive — form the basis of Atkinson's achievement motivation model based on the cognitive process of expectancy. Expectancy is described as a 'cognitive anticipation' that the performance of some act will be followed by a particular consequence: the expectancy that effort will lead to success. The incentive represents the value a person places on task success. The incentive can take the form of reward or punishment, either the achievement of the task, or the negative feelings associated with non-achievement. The third variable, motive, is the underlying drive to strive to satisfy a valued need (a need for achievement). Atkinson proposed that an individual's tendency to approach a task was determined by three elements (Figure 3.2):

— Motive to achieve success (Motive to Achieve), or a motive to avoid failure,

MOTIVE → EXPECTANCY → INCENTIVE

Motive to achieve success   Motive to avoid failure   Perceived expectancy of task success   Incentive value of task success

Adapted from Atkinson (1966) by ESSEC ISIS (2010)

Figure 3.2   Atkinson's achievement expectancy model.

[17]Murray, H (1938). *Explorations in Personality*. New York: Oxford University Press, p. 164.

[18]Atkinson, JW and NT Feather (1966). *A Theory of Achievement Motivation*. New York: Wiley.

[19]Atkinson, JW (1964). *Introduction to Motivation*. Princeton, NJ: Van Nostrand.

— Expectancy (perceived probability) of task success,
— Incentive value of task success.

Role in the organisation today

Atkinson's achievement motivation model is useful for understanding and motivating high-achievers in the organisation and is important for understanding that some individuals are more driven than others by a motive for success and achievement.[20]

There are several lessons to be learned in the application of achievement motivation at the workplace today. First, feedback is pivotal to communicating to the employee what constitutes optimal performance. Second, high-achievers prefer job profiles that carry personal responsibility, provide feedback and have a degree of risk; they tend to be successful in entrepreneurial activities such as running their own businesses, managing self-contained units within a large organisation and in sales positions. Employees can be trained to stimulate their achievement need.[21]

Achievement motivation highlights the interactional role of the organisation in enabling high-achievers to reach their full potential by providing opportunities for achievement of optimally challenging goals, and feedback.[22]

Organisational Application

Many studies have been undertaken on the effect of achievement motivation training on managers, particularly in small businesses; it has been successfully applied to entrepreneurs or executives to encourage success and has been found in the majority of cases to improve the performance of the company.[23]

Leaders such as Bill Gates of Microsoft and Steve Jobs of Apple can be identified as having a high need for achievement, which is the driver behind their high performance and continuous success.

---

[20]Atkinson, JW and NT Feather (1966). *A Theory of Achievement Motivation.* New York: Wiley; Weiner, B (1974). *Achievement Motivation and Attribution Theory.* Morristown, NJ: General Learning Press.
[21]Stahl, MJ (1983). Achievement, power, and managerial motivation: Selecting managerial talent with the job choice exercise. *Personnel Psychology*, Winter, 775–790.
[22]McClelland, D (1961). *The Achieving Society.* Princeton, NJ: Nostrand.
[23]Miron, D and DC McClelland (1979). The impact of achievement motivation training on small businesses. *California Management Review*, 21(4), 13–28.

Lessons Learned

Achievement motivation refers to the concept of being motivated *to achieve*, characterised by the motivation to perform tasks well (high standard of accomplishment), the desire to undertake new and challenging tasks (mastery) and the desire to surpass the performance of others (competitiveness). Feedback, challenge and autonomy are key factors that help to nurture an organisation's high-achievers.

3.2.3. *Motivation by Expectancy: Attribution*

Developed by Bernard Weiner (1972).

Overview

Attribution theory is concerned with the reasons people attribute to their successes and failures, and accordingly the effect of these attributions on future behaviour. Although not an all-encompassing theory of motivation at work, it is still an important piece of the motivational puzzle and has implications on motivational behaviour.[24]

Past behaviour has an impact on the expectancy for task success, or failure, in future behaviour. The locus of causality, which refers to the belief that behaviour is caused internally (by forces within the person), or externally (by forces in the person's environment), leads a person to make causal explanations (attributions) about past behaviour. The causal behaviours fall into four causal categories: ability, effort, task difficulty, and luck. Effort and ability attributions are internal control explanations while task difficulty and luck represent external control explanations.[25]

Individuals filter information gained from performance feedback and rewards through three causal attribution dimensions:

— Locus of causality: refers to the extent to which outcomes are perceived as internally or externally mediated (e.g., *Am I responsible for the outcome of this task?*).
— Stability of outcomes: refers to the extent to which outcomes are viewed as enduring across time and situations (e.g., *Is this a permanent or a changeable outcome?*).

---

[24] Weiner, B (1974). *Achievement Motivation and Attribution Theory.* Morristown, NJ: General Learning Press.
[25] Weiner, B (1980). *Human Motivation.* New York: Holt, Rinehart & Winston.

— Perceived controllability: refers to the extent to which outcomes are perceived to be under volitional control (e.g., *Was I instructed to complete this task or did I have the freedom to complete it as I thought fit?*).

Task failure attributed to unstable causes (effort or bad luck) has been shown to be positively related to higher expectations for subsequent performance. Conversely, attributions to stable causes (task difficulty and ability) following failure are associated with lower expectancy for future performance; for instance, an individual who attributes a task failure to ability may have a low expectation for task success in similar tasks in the future. In the case of task success, attributions to stable factors enhance future performance expectancy; attributions to unstable causes tend to lower performance expectancy.[26]

Role in the organisation today

Attribution theory can be used to explain the difference in motivation between high and low achievers. Achievement-motivated individuals tend to attribute their successes to their own efforts and their failures to not trying hard enough. If they fail they are likely to try again because they tend to believe that with greater effort they can succeed. Thus, they consistently perceive their ability levels as being quite high. When they do succeed it is because they tried hard and used their abilities.[27] It is useful for managing and understanding ineffective behaviour behind task failure and may help managers affect positive change in behaviour (Figure 3.3).[28]

People with a low need for achievement view effort as irrelevant. They attribute their failure to other factors, in particular lack of ability. In their view, success is a consequence of the external factors of easy tasks and luck. Training to bring about motivational change in achievement should first focus on teaching that individual effort impacts task success and internal causality plays a key role in the level of performance on a task.

---

[26]Weiner, B and J Sierad (1975). Misattribution for failure and enhancement of achievement strivings. *Journal of Personality and Social Psychology*, 31, 415–421.

[27]Weiner, B, R Nierenberg and M Goldstein (1976). Social learning (locus of control) versus attributional (causal stability) interpretations of expectancy of success. *Journal of Personality*, 44, 52–68.

[28]Weiner, B (1974). *Achievement Motivation and Attribution Theory*. Morristown, NJ: General Learning Press.

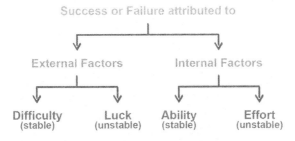

Figure 3.3   Attribution theory.

Understanding the reasons behind task failure can help the manager to take corrective action.[29]

Organisational Application

Attributions of Success or Failure in Sales

A new salesperson who fails to persuade a client to purchase a product may perceive this failure as the result of inadequate preparation (internal, unstable and controllable). In this instance, the perception of the cause being something within his control to change for future situations should lead the salesperson to be hopeful for expectations of success with future clients. Performance motivation is likely to be enhanced in the next sales attempt.[30]

Conversely, in the case of long-tenured employees who repeatedly fail to close a sale, they are more likely to attribute the cause of failure to a lack of ability (internal, stable and uncontrollable). In this instance, the employee is more likely to anticipate repeated failure in the future, hopelessness and lower self-esteem. All of these factors would be expected to result in a lower motivation to perform in the future.

---

[29] Weiner, B, R Nierenberg and M Goldstein (1976). Social learning (locus of control) versus attributional (causal stability) interpretations of expectancy of success. *Journal of Personality*, 44, 52–68.

[30] Kanfer, R (1990). Motivation theory and industrial and organizational psychology. In *Handbook of Industrial and Organizational Psychology*, MD Dunnette and LD Hough (eds.), pp. 75–170. Palo Alto, CA: Consulting Psychologists Press.

Lessons Learned

Attribution theory is concerned with the reasons people attribute to their successes and failures, and accordingly the effect of these attributions on future behaviour. The causal explanations (attributions) for past behaviour fall into four causal categories: ability, effort, task difficulty and luck. The attribution of success or failure to these four factors has a varying impact on the expectancy for task success, or failure, in future behaviour. An understanding of individual attributions can help the manager to affect positive changes though attitudinal change of employees.

3.3. Motivation by Learning

Learning also plays a role in shaping employee behaviour in the workplace; people tend to learn quickly which type of behaviours are rewarded and which are undesired. Learning causes behaviour to be modified or adjusted based on direct or indirect past experience and thus plays an important role in maintaining motivated behaviour.[31] Freud also spoke about how anticipated pleasure or pain determines future responses (Figure 3.4).

Decisions concerning present or future behaviours are largely influenced by the consequences of rewards associated with past behaviour, referred to as hedonism of the past. Past actions that led to positive outcomes would tend to be repeated, whereas past actions that led to negative outcomes would tend to lessen. People learn from the outcomes of past behaviour.

Adapted from Bandura (2001) by ESSEC ISIS (2010)

Figure 3.4   Learning and behaviour.

---

[31]Bandura, A (2001). Social cognitive theory: An agentic perspective. *Annual Review of Psychology*, 52, 1–26.

3.3.1. *Learning by Reinforcement and Rewards*

Developed by B.F. Skinner (1957).

Overview

Motivation by reinforcement suggests that voluntary or learned behaviour is a function of its consequences. Behaviour that results in pleasant consequences is more likely to be repeated, and behaviour that results in unpleasant consequences is less likely to be repeated. Reinforcement theory, like expectancy theory, also suggests that in any given situation people will explore a variety of possible behaviours and make choices when deciding to pursue one course of action or task over another; these choices are affected by the consequences of earlier behaviours. It assumes that people explore different behaviours and systematically choose those that result in the most desirable outcomes. The consequences of behaviour are called reinforcement (Figure 3.5).[32]

In the organisation, managers can use various types of reinforcement to guide employee behaviour. There are four basic forms of reinforcement: positive reinforcement, avoidance, extinction, and punishment.[33] The two most widely used types of reinforcement are positive reinforcement (reward) and punishment, in layman's terms.[34] Positive reinforcement, or

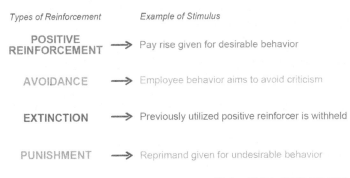

Adapted from Hamner, Luthans and Kreitner (1970) by ESSEC ISIS (2010)

Figure 3.5   Motivation by reinforcement.

---

[32]Skinner, BF (1974). *About Behaviorism*; Skinner, BF, *The Behavior of Organisms. An Experimental Analysis.* New York: Appleton-Century-Crofts.

[33]Arvey, R and JM Ivancevich (1980). Punishment in organizations: A review, propositions, and research suggestions. *Acadamy of Management Review*, April, 123–132.

[34]Michale, J (2005). Positive and negative reinforcement, a distinction that is no longer necessary; or a better way to talk about bad things. *Journal of Organizational Behavior Management*, 24.

reward, motivates employees to maintain or increase the frequency of that behaviour. A salary increase following a period of high performance, or a compliment from the manager following successful completion of a task, are examples of positive reinforcement. Punishment is an unpleasant or aversive consequence of behaviour. Many instances of unpleasant consequences in life teach us by means of punishment: getting wet after going out in the rain or suffering a hangover after drinking too much. We often learn to change our behaviour as a result.[35]

Role in the organisation today

Reinforcement theory suggests that desirable behaviours can be encouraged by linking those behaviours with positive consequences, and undesirable behaviours can be discouraged by linking them with negative consequences. In the organisation, positive reinforcement is used to encourage desirable behaviours in employees; positive reinforcement may be in the form of praise, recognition, financial reward, pay rise and so on.[36]

Although positive reinforcement is widely used in the organisation, managers should be careful to ensure that the use of rewards is not perceived as controlling. Negative reinforcement (punishment) should be carefully administered, and it should not be used inappropriately or too often as employee morale could suffer.[37]

Organisational Application

Reinforcement

Proper management of reinforcement can be used to shape behaviour in work by influencing the direction, level and persistence of an individual's behaviour. There are many examples of reinforcement in the workplace: a real-estate agent paid partially on commission understands that high income is contingent on generating house sales; a position for a trainee accountant is contingent on passing in-house company examinations; positive feedback from a manager on a task performance leads an employee to exert effort for similar tasks in the future; the

---

[35]Moorhead, G and RW Griffen (2004). *Organizational Behavior, Managing People and Organizations*. Boston: Houghton Mifflin Company.
[36]Luthans, F and R Kreitner (1975). *Organizational Behavior Modification*. Glenview, IL: Scott, Foresman.
[37]Moorhead, G and RW Griffen (2004). *Organizational Behavior, Managing People and Organizations*. Boston: Houghton Mifflin Company.

incentive of promotion leads an engineer to exert high efforts to perform. The rewarding of progress through recognition, positive feedback or tangible rewards in an organisation contributes to the reinforcement of positive performance. However, organisations need to be careful that reinforcement is not perceived as controlling.

Organisational Application

High performance in GE, under its former CEO Jack Welch, was encouraged through a combination of factors, one of which was a ranking system. Welch required managers to divide talent into three groups: the top 20%, the middle 70%, and the bottom 10%, many of whom were shown the door due to inadequate performance or potential. This prospective of job loss represented a reinforcement that taught employees to perform to a high level. However, this practice is carefully managed in GE and is not intended to create a culture of fear: Jack Welch believes that if people are not performing well it is because they are in the wrong job, and you are doing them a favour by being candid with them. According to Jack Welch, 'candid appraisals are the most important'. You need to tell your people 'here's what I like about what you're doing and here's where you can improve. A manager's obligation is to make sure your people know exactly where they stand'.[38] The 'stick' approach to employees is not advised today as it negatively affects engagement over the long term.

A study by Steve Scullen, an associate professor of management at Drake University in Des Moines, found that 'forced ranking', including the firing of the bottom 5% or 10%, results in a 16% improvement in productivity; however, this improvement is valid only over the first couple of years. After the initial peak in productivity the gains decrease, from 16% in the first two years, down to just a 6% increase in the third and fourth years to almost no gains in year 10. It is clear that negative reinforcement (avoidance) such as that practiced in GE must be carefully managed in order to balance long-term employee engagement and performance with potential productivity gains.[39]

---

[38] Jack Welch on Differentiation (Video). *Businessweek*; http://feedroom.businessweek.com/?fr_story=7441b25b0993b6a46975a798b6c3e2abf6cbe492
[39] The struggle to measure performance (6 January 2006). *Business Week*.

Lessons Learned

Motivation by reinforcement, suggests that voluntary or learned behaviour is a function of its consequences. Behaviour that leads to pleasant consequences is more likely to be repeated, and behaviour leads to unpleasant consequences is less likely to be repeated. Proper management of reinforcement can be used to shape behaviour in work by influencing the direction, level, and persistence of an individual's behaviour through four forms of reinforcement: positive reinforcement, avoidance (negative reinforcement), extinction and punishment. Reinforcement should be balanced with consideration for employee needs and should not be overly controlling.

3.3.2. *Social Learning*

Developed by Albert Bandura (1963).

Overview

Social learning occurs when people observe the behaviours of others in their environment and recognise the consequences of their behaviour, and alter their own behaviour as a result. Social learning influences motivation at work in several ways: many of the behaviours we exhibit in our daily work lives are learned by 'cues' from others at the workplace; in other words, people learn about accepted standards of behaviour by observing the conduct, outcomes or consequences, and characteristics of others in specific situations (Figure 3.6).[40]

> 'If knowledge and skills could be acquired only through direct experience, the process of human development would be greatly retarded, not to mention exceedingly tedious, costly, and hazardous. Fortunately, people can expand their knowledge and skills on the basis of information conveyed by modeling influences.' — Albert Bandura[41]

The observational learning or modelling process has four main steps: attention (paying attention to the key information), retention (remembering

---

[40]Bandura, A (1977). *Social Learning Theory*. Englewood Cliffs, NJ: Prentice-Hall.
[41]Wood, R and A Bandura (1989). Social cognitive theory of organizational management. *The Academy of Management Review*, 14(3), 361–384.

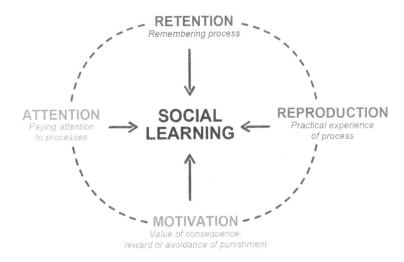

Adapted from Bandura (1989) by ESSEC ISIS (2010)

Figure 3.6   Social learning.

the key processes), reproduction (practical experience of the task improves learning) and motivation (people attach a value to the consequences, such as a reward or avoidance of punishment).[42]

Role in the organisation today

Social learning is useful for setting standards of behaviour and creating an organisational culture that values some behaviours over others. It is important to recognise the importance of the organisational environment and culture in shaping an employee's behaviour. The standards set by the group of employees will provide cues for new employees; for example, a new employee will learn through cues from fellow workers about the dress code, degree of formality between the ranks, etc. Several environmental conditions must exist for social learning to take place: first, the behaviour being observed must be relatively simple; a complicated technical procedure

---

[42]Wood, R and A Bandura (1989). Social cognitive theory of organizational management. *The Academy of Management Review*, 14(3), 361–384.

is not so easily learnt by observation. Second, the behaviour must not be of an intellectual nature; writing computer software or thinking abstractly cannot easily be learnt through observation. Finally, one must possess the physical ability to execute the task.[43]

Organisational Application

Certain behaviours can be taught to employees through videos and by giving specific behavioural cues to encourage desired behaviours. Transparent rewards or recognition given to an employee for innovative ideas will demonstrate to employees the type of behaviour that is valued.

Lessons Learned

Social learning occurs when people observe the behaviours of others in their environment, evaluate the consequences of such behaviour and alter their own behaviour as a result. Social learning influences motivation at work in several ways: many of the behaviours we exhibit in our daily work lives are learned by 'cues' from others in the workplace. It is important to recognise the importance of the organisational environment and culture in shaping the employee's behaviour.

3.4. Summary of the Processes of Motivation at Work

While the needs theories, the 'building blocks', evaluate the different needs that stimulate consequent behaviour, the process theories examine how precisely people make personal choices about which behaviours to pursue based on their expectation of outcomes and based on learned responses from past experience.

3.4.1. *Summary of the Expectancy Processes of Motivation*

The expectancy of a particular outcome (performance outcome and reward outcome) plays a key role in the choice of behaviour that an individual pursues at work. Thus, the motivation of an individual is influenced

---

[43] Moorhead, G and RW Griffen (2004). *Organizational Behavior, Managing People and Organizations*. Boston: Houghton Mifflin Company.

by expectancies — performance outcomes (task success, achievement, or failure) and reward outcomes (rewards such as praise or monetary rewards).

Expectancy Motivation Concept	Summary	Role in Motivation at Work
Expectancies: Values and Rewards Victor Vroom, 1964 Porter and Lawlor, 1968	People will engage in motivated behaviour if they believe their efforts will lead to performance (expectancy), believe that their performance will be rewarded (instrumentality), and if they value the expected rewards (valence).	Rewards can be used most effectively if the manager understands the different values individual employees place on rewards. Feedback should always be used to communicate on desirable performance.
Achievement Henry Murray, 1938 McClelland, 1953 John Atkinson, 1966	Achievement motivation arises from an acquired (learned) need for achievement: the motivation to perform tasks well, the desire to undertake new and challenging tasks and the desire to surpass the performance of others.	In the workplace people seek success and avoid failure. Organisations can help high-achievers to reach their full potential by providing opportunities for achievement of optimally challenging goals and feedback.
Attribution Weiner, 1972	Attribution is concerned with the reasons people attribute to their successes and failures, and the influence of these causal explanations (ability, effort, task difficulty, and luck) on future behaviour.	The conclusions a worker draws concerning the reasons for past success or failure on a project will impact the expectancy for task success or failure in future instances.

3.4.2. *Summary of the Learning Processes of Motivation*

Learning also plays a role in shaping employee behaviour in the workplace; people tend to learn quickly which type of behaviours are rewarded and which are undesired. Learning causes behaviour to be modified or adjusted based on direct or indirect past experience and thus plays an important role in maintaining motivated behaviour.

Learning Motivation Concept	Summary	Role in Motivation at Work
Reinforcement B. F. Skinner, 1957	Motivation by reinforcement suggests that voluntary or learned behaviour is a function of its consequences. Behaviour that leads to pleasant consequences is more likely to be repeated, and behaviour leads to unpleasant consequences is less likely to be repeated.	When properly managed, reinforcement can be used to shape behaviour in work by influencing the direction, level, and persistence of an individual's behaviour through four forms of reinforcement: positive reinforcement, avoidance (negative reinforcement), extinction, and punishment. Reinforcement should be balanced with consideration for employee needs and should not be overly controlling.
Social Learning Albert Bandura, 1963	Social learning occurs when people observe the behaviours of others in their environment, evaluate the consequences of such behaviour, and alter their own behaviour as a result.	Social learning influences motivation at work in several ways: many of the behaviours we exhibit in our daily work lives are learned by 'cues' from others in the workplace. It is important to recognise the importance of the organisational environment and culture in shaping the employee's behaviour.

Chapter 4

THE ARCHITECTURE OF MOTIVATION AT WORK

This chapter examines the peripheral factors that influence motivation in the workplace. The guiding processes such as the supportive framework of the organisation, goal-setting and the use of transparent and fair processes are inextricably linked to the commitment and motivation of the employee. The Architecture of Motivation is also concerned with individual specificities such as personality, generation and culture that explain why motivation differs from one person to another and from one culture to another.

Motivation at work is an intricate puzzle composed of the *building blocks* (the needs that act as a stimulus for action); the *processes* (the cognitive choices that translate needs into action); and finally, the *architecture*. 'The Architecture of Motivation at Work' does not lie at the heart of the motivation puzzle, but is concerned with moderators of motivation such as the leadership style, the stage of life of the employees, individual personalities and the diversity of cultures; these factors unquestionably play a role in influencing motivation and performance in the organisation.

4.1. Overview of the Chapter

First we examine the role of management in motivating the workforce. The leaders, and the policies and practices designed by leaders, are inextricably linked to the motivation of the employees of the organisation.

In the examination of the relationship between management structures and motivation, we study the styles of management that impact attitudes and behaviour; examine the value of goal-setting; and look at the importance of treating employees with fairness and procedural justice.

Subsequently, we look at the individual specificities that cause employee behaviour to be heterogeneous across employee groups. Personality, culture and generation create different employee profiles and require a certain measure of adaption and personalisation from one employee to another.

4.1.1. *Glossary of Key Definitions for 'Architecture of Motivation at Work'*

Culture: It is the collective programming of the mind that distinguishes the members of one group or category of people from another. Culture is learned, and not inherited. It derives from one's social environment, and not from one's genes.

Goals: Goals are desired end states or aspirations for the future. They play a causal role in action; setting goals improves an individual's focus on the tasks that are most important and gives more clarity on how to prioritise tasks.

Personality: An individual's characteristic patterns of thought, emotion and behaviour, together with the psychological mechanisms behind those patterns.

4.2. A Supportive Framework

The style of management and the supportive framework of the organisation can have a profound impact on the morale of workers, and the willingness of the employees to strive for the organisational goals of the company. A manager who is liked, revered or feared can have a spectacular impact on an individual's engagement or willingness to work towards the achievement of organisational goals. More than ever, managers are paying attention to individual employee needs because they realise the value of each individual to the organisation as a whole. A formal process of goal-setting, performance review and appraisals ensures that employees know what they are doing right and where they can develop further. A two-way communication and goal-setting process is an important framework for motivation. It can help employees to develop, improve competencies and derive satisfaction from the completion of tasks and to ensure that individual goals are aligned with those of the company.

4.2.1. Management Styles

Developed by Douglas McGregor (1960).

Overview

The style of management can have a profound impact on the morale of workers, and the willingness of the employees to strive for the organisational goals of the company. Douglas McGregor, a theorist, examined the effects of two different management styles on employee motivation. At the time of development of his motivation model, Theory X and Theory Y, in the 1960s, McGregor believed that organisations and management methods of the time generally corresponded to what he termed the 'Theory X' model of management. This form of management was governed by the assumption that human beings by nature have little ambition, dislike work, want to avoid responsibility and need to be closely supervised in order to work effectively. This corresponds with the Taylorist view of management of the time, which was characterised by repetitive work driven by piecemeal incentives designed to increase efficiencies, but which did not consider an employee's higher-order needs. Although this method may have been successful on a short-term basis, it ultimately led to situations of reduced motivation; and in some cases, it ignited a form of worker rebellion, resulting in restrictions of output, antagonism towards management, militant unionism and a discord with management objectives.[1]

Instead, McGregor advocated a shift towards a 'Theory Y' practice of management. This management practice suggests that a potential for development, a capacity for assuming responsibility and a readiness to direct behaviour towards organisational goals are characteristics present in all workers.[2]

McGregor argued that organisational environments that provide employees with opportunities to satisfy their higher-order needs will encourage effective performance. He said that each employee can make a vital contribution to the company, and so they should be listened to. Otherwise, when employees are ignored and ill-treated by management, and denied opportunities for development, employees begin to resent management; this in turn tends to have a reductive effect on motivation (Figure 4.1).[3]

---

[1] McGregor, D (1960). *The Human Side of Enterprise*. New York: McGraw-Hill.
[2] Vroom, VH and EL Deci (1970). *Management and Motivation*. Baltimore: Penguin Education.
[3] McGregor, D (1960). *The Human Side of Enterprise*. New York: McGraw-Hill.

THEORY X
Rigid control of employees,
no responsibility or intrinsic motivation,
"stick" approach,
no development opportunities.

EMPLOYEE

Empowering,
positive.

Controlling,
authoritarian.

THEORY Y
A person's higher level needs represent
an important motivational force.
An open management method
that gives employees responsibility,
autonomy and opportunities for growth.

EMPLOYEE

Adapted from McGregor (1960) by ESSEC ISIS (2010)

Figure 4.1   Motivation by management styles: Theory X and Theory Y.

McGregor's Theory Y Approach to Management contends that:

- The potential for motivation and development, the capacity to assume responsibility and the willingness to direct behaviour towards organisational goals are present in all people; it is the responsibility of management to make it possible for staff to recognise and develop these characteristics for themselves.
- The essential task of management is to arrange working conditions so that employees can achieve their own goals best by self-directing their efforts towards organisational goals.

Organisational Application

Styles of Management: Andy Pearson, PepsiCo

The management style transformation of Andy Pearson represents a move from a Theory X style of management to a Theory Y. It highlights the importance of a good leader in creating an organisational culture whereby workers are valued and enjoy being part of the company.

In 1980, as CEO of PepsiCo, Andy Pearson, was named one of the 10 toughest bosses in America. The old Andy Pearson was responsible for driving revenues from $1 billion to $8 billion at PepsiCo with a management style that thrived on the creation of fear and was described as being 'brutally abrasive'. Every year he fired the least productive 10% to 20% of his workforce.

Despite the success of his demanding style, he developed a new way to lead based on employee recognition and value. His new style emphasises guidance, as opposed to control. Control restricts creativity and satisfaction over the long term. His opinion on this change in management style: 'If I could only unleash the power of everybody in the organisation, instead of just a few people, what could we accomplish? We'd be a much better company.'[4]

Lessons Learned

Management styles have a profound impact on employee motivation, morale and the success of the organisation. McGregor draws attention to the benefits of positive leadership styles that encourage responsibility and growth through the development of his Theory Y of leadership. Theory Y assumes that the potential for motivation and development, the capacity to assume responsibility, and the willingness to direct behaviour towards organisational goals are present in all people as opposed to the controlling, coercive methods of Theory X which stifle the human needs for growth and esteem.

4.2.2. *Setting Goals*

Developed by Edwin Locke and Gary Latham (1981).

Overview

Goal-setting refers to the process of setting goals to motivate employees to increase or improve their performance. Locke proposed that goals are the most powerful determinant of task behaviour and motivation at the workplace. Goal-setting suggests that goals (desired end states or aspirations for the future) play a causal role in action. A goal can be described as 'the object or aim of an action, for example, to attain a specific standard of proficiency, usually within a specified time limit,' and conscious goals are thus expected to positively affect action.[5]

---

[4]Dorset, D (2001). *Andy Pearson Finds Love*, in Fast Company, July 31, 2001; http://www.fastcompany.com/magazine/49/pearson.html.
[5]Locke, EA and GP Latham (2002). Building a practically useful theory of goal setting and task motivation: A 35-year odyssey. *American Psychologist*, 57(9), 705–717.

Most of the concepts of motivation are based on the understanding that people initiate and persist at behaviours to the extent that they believe the behaviours will lead to desired outcomes or goals. Tolman (1932) described humans as purpose-driven animals.[6] Ryan (1970) observed that human behaviour was inherently guided by intentions, tasks, conscious purpose or goals.[7]

How do goals drive motivation?

Locke looked at the question of why some people perform better in work tasks than others and concluded that although the explanation lies partly in individual variations in ability, knowledge and methods; the answer lies in the fact that people have different goals. People aim for different outcomes when performing a task. Goal-related action does not have to be conscious at all times in order for it to regulate action; once a main goal is set, action is frequently guided by a series of sub-goals, which lead to the achievement of the over-arching goal.[8]

Goals affect performance through three motivational mechanisms: choice, effort and persistence. A specific goal facilitates choice by encouraging attitudes that are relevant to achieving a goal and by discouraging those that are not goal relevant. In short, goal-setting improves an individual's focus on the tasks that are most important and gives more clarity on how to prioritise tasks.[9]

A goal serves as a motivator because it causes people to compare their present capacity to perform with that required to succeed at the goal and thereby causing stimulation or an increase in performance. When an individual believes he will fall short of a goal, he will feel dissatisfied and will work harder to attain it, but only if he feels that it is possible to attain. When an individual succeeds at meeting a goal, he feels competent, successful and experiences a sense of achievement.[10]

People set goals concerning their future behaviours and these goals influence actual behaviours. Having a goal causes the person to develop

---

[6]Tolman, EC (1932). *Purposive Behavior in Animals and Men.* New York: Century Co.
[7]Ryan, TA (1970). *Intentional Behavior.* New York: Ronald Press.
[8]Locke, EA and GP Latham (2002). Building a practically useful theory of goal setting and task motivation: A 35-year odyssey. *American Psychologist*, 57(9), 705–717.
[9]Seijts, G (2001). Setting goals when performance doesn't matter. *Ivey Business Journal* January/February 2001.
[10]Locke, EA, KN Shaw, LM Saari and GP Latham (1981). Goal setting and task performance: 1969–1980. *Psychological Bulletin*, 90(1), 125–152.

Figure 4.2   Motivation by goal-setting.

strategies to attain the goal and hence influences problem-solving. Goals affect performance by directing attention, regulating effort, increasing persistence and encouraging goal attainment strategies.[11]

Task-goal attributes influencing goal attainment

According to Locke *et al.* (1981), a review of both laboratory and field studies on the effects of setting goals when performing a task found that in 90% of the studies, specific and challenging goals lead to higher performance than easy goals, 'do your best' goals, or no goals.[12]

Organisational Application

The former CEO of General Electric, Jack Welsh, required goals and stretch-goals to be set throughout the organisation in order to achieve GE's leadership position and to drive growth, inspired by his readings from a 19th century Prussian war General. Welch preached a philosophy he called 'planful opportunism', whereby GE employees were given an over-reaching stretch-goal and permitted to do whatever it took to reach

---

[11]Steers, RM and LW Porter (1974). The role of task-goal attributes in employee performance. *Psychological Bulletin*, 81, 434–452.
[12]Locke, EA, KN Shaw, LM Saari and GP Latham (1981). Goal setting and task performance: 1969–1980. *Psychological Bulletin*, 90(1), 125–152.

the target. Even if employees did not reach the target, the stretch goal motivated people to increase their performance.[13]

According to Locke and Latham, people with high self-efficacy set higher goals than do people with lower self-efficacy, are more committed to assigned goals, find and use better task strategies to attain the goals and respond more positively to negative feedback than do people with low self-efficacy. Self-efficacy refers to the belief that one has the capabilities to execute the courses of actions required to successfully perform the task to attain the set goal. It relates to both inherent personal beliefs regarding ability, and also past experiences relating to mastery of a task.

Example

A study by the University of Cologne (2008) found that golfers who were told that their ball was a 'lucky ball' were 35% more likely to sink a putt than the control group. The belief that it was a lucky ball increased their confidence and self-efficacy, that is, their belief that they would sink the putt, and higher self-efficacy increases one's likelihood of success.

Goal-setting is more effective when feedback allows performance to be monitored in relation to an individual's goals. Goals provide a yardstick for employees to measure and evaluate their own efforts against their actual performance, and feedback provides a yardstick with which to measure individual perceptions of performance against those of the supervisor. Feedback prevents a diminution in performance as well as encouraging a steady improvement over time.[14]

Role in the organisation today

The effectiveness of goal-setting as a motivational method has been widely proven. Goal-setting can be used to motivate employees to perform well and also to ensure that individual performance is in line with the strategic objectives of the company. Employees play an integral role in the attainment of organisational goals and without clear goals, feedback, reward and

---

[13]Dulberg *et al.* *Jack Welsh and the Motivation of GE*. Chicago: The University of Chicago Graduate School of Business.

[14]Steers, RM (1984). *Introduction to Organizational Behavior*, 2nd Ed. Glenview, IL: Scott, Foresman.

recognition for goal attainment employees will lose direction under the ambiguity of the leaders' strategy. Reinforcement also fosters motivation towards goal attainment; a person who is rewarded or recognised for achieving a goal will be more inclined to strive towards the next difficult goal.

Goal-setting is a widely used technique in organisations today. Most sales departments use goals in the form of sales quotas to motivate employees. Goals are present in many forms in organisations: a budget is a monetary-guided goal; a quota is a standard to be met; and a deadline is a time-guided goal. The use of SMART goal-setting is advocated in organisations today: Specific, Measureable, Attainable, Relevant and Time-bound.[15]

Organisational Application

Kaizen

The Kaizen method of goal-setting is used by Japanese companies such as Toyota. This method involves incrementally increasing the difficulty of goals over time and encouraging a philosophy of continual improvement. Companies such as Toyota have demonstrated that this form of management can be successfully implemented in both Japanese and American cultural environments. Many companies have attempted to emulate this management style due to the evident influence on company's success.[16]

Management by Objectives

Management by Objectives (MBO) is a system of motivating and integrating the efforts of business managers by setting goals for the organisation as a whole and then linking these objectives down through each management level, so that goal attainment at each level helps attain goals at the next-highest level and ultimately feeds into the overall goals of the organisation.[17]

---

[15]Doran, GT (1981). There's a S.M.A.R.T. way to write managements's goals and objectives. *Management Review*, 70(11), 35–36.
[16]Winfield, I and M Kerrin (1996). Toyota motor manufacturing in Europe: Lessons for management development. *Journal of Management Development*, 15(4), 49–56.
[17]Drucker, PF (1954). *The Practice of Management*. London: Elsevier.

Lessons Learned

Goal-setting is one of the most effective and widely used methods of guiding motivation in the organisation today. Goals help individuals to achieve their personal goals through the achievement of tasks, and provide the individual with a clear view of organisational strategy and vision. Goals influence performance by directing attention, regulating effort, increasing persistence and encouraging goal attainment strategies. A goal serves as a motivator because it causes people to compare their present capacity to perform with that required to succeed at the goal and thereby stimulating an increase in performance and problem-solving strategies, that is, goals serve as a yardstick for improvement in performance for both managers and employees.

4.2.3. *Fairness in the Workplace*

Developed by J.S. Adams (1967); Jerald Greenberg (1987).

Overview

A fair workplace helps maintain employee commitment, contributes to job satisfaction and minimises absenteeism and turnover. The way that people measure fairness is at the heart of Equity Theory. Employees evaluate their treatment in terms of inputs (what they put into the job) and outputs (what they receive in return for the job) and compare this evaluation to their 'reference group'. Employees arrive at their perception of fairness (equity) by comparing the balance of the inputs they contribute (work effort and skills) and the outputs they receive (rewards, pay) with the input–output balance received by other people deemed to be relevant reference groups. Perceptions of inequitable treatment may lead to dissatisfaction and demotivation.[18]

Greenberg complemented Equity Theory by building on organisational justice concepts. He suggested that when assessing the fairness of organisational decisions (e.g. the allocation of pay and other resources), employees take into account not only what those decisions are (i.e., outcomes, such as

---

[18]Adams, JS (1965). Inequity in social exchange. *Advances in Experimental and Social Psychology*, 62, 335–343.

pay and performance ratings), but also the manner in which those decisions are made (e.g. procedures).

Role in the organisation today

Maintaining an equitable and transparent system is key to establishing perceptions of fairness in the organisation, which helps maintain employee commitment and contributes to job satisfaction.

In the organisation, a common source of inequity perception is employee remuneration. Although revealing all of the salaries of employees within the company is not considered beneficial, one study states that clear communication on how compensation plans are established, evaluated and allocated is important for establishing a code of fairness.[19]

Organisational Application

In 1982, General Motors negotiated wage concessions from its unionised employees and then announced that executives would receive large bonuses. The employee outrage that ensued led General Motors to cancel the bonuses.[20]

In another case, a pharmaceutical firm was taken to court and sued for pay differentials between male and female colleagues on the same level. Pay differentials, bonuses and other rewards represent an important lever of motivation; however, if pay differentials are used by the company a fair and transparent system of attainment must exist in the organisation.[21]

Lessons Learned

Maintaining an equitable and transparent system is key to establishing perceptions of fairness in the organisation which plays an important role in creating employee satisfaction.

4.3.   Considering Individual Specificities

Motivation alone cannot explain why some people work faster or more efficiently than others. Innate characteristics, ability, past experience,

---

[19] Wagner, R and J Harter (2006). The problem of pay. *Gallup Management Journal.*
[20] Freeman, RB and JL Medoff (1984). *What Do Unions Do?* New York: Basic Books.
[21] Freeman, RB and JL Medoff (1984). *What Do Unions Do?* New York: Basic Books.

generation or age, and even the culture one grows up in, all influence motivation and performance. One can only perform according to the limits of one's capabilities.

As William Revelle notes, cutting across all of the central factors contributing to motivation are the effects of individual difference such as personality, on motivation and performance.[22] One of the key lessons for organisations today is the need to understand individual differences, values and needs and to adapt motivational techniques according to the person.

4.3.1. Stage of Life

Overview

Today's workforce faces a growing need to hold onto or attract older workers in order to moderate the effects of declining populations and a worker shortage created by the retirement of a large segment of the workforce: the baby boomers. Holding onto older workers, with valuable experience and knowledge, as well as attracting younger generations to the organisation, entails an understanding of the unique needs of the different generations within the workforce.[23]

Understanding the needs of different generations is instrumental in developing motivational practices that are appropriate and effective. There is an increasing need for 'mass personalisation' in terms of autonomy, variety and flexibility; as one expert argues 'it's matching it more to where a person is in their life, so when you're at one stage, you might take time off for education and travel.... and later, when you're winding down, you might not have to work such long hours[24]'.

The idiosyncrasies of different generations

In today's workforce four generations work side-by-side: Veterans or Pre-Boomers, Baby Boomers, Generation X and Generation Y.[25] Extensive research on generational differences has revealed a unique set of attitudes that characterise each generation, suggesting important implications on

---

[22]Revelle, W (1987). Personality and motivation: Sources of inefficiency in cognitive performance. *Journal of Research in Personality*, 21(4), 436–452.

[23]Economic Intelligence Unit (2008). Talent Wars, the struggle for tomorrow's workforce.

[24]Economic Intelligence Unit (2008). Talent Wars, the struggle for tomorrow's workforce.

[25]Manpower (2007). Generation Y in the Workplace Australia; http://www.manpower. cz/images/GenerationYintheWorkplace.pdf.

the employer–employee relationship and motivation.[26] In the United States there is an estimated 80 million baby boomers, 78 million millennials and just 46 million generation Xers.[27]

	Category	% of World Population[29]
Generational Distinctions[28]	Pre 1946: Veterans or Pre-Boomers	4.67%
	1947–1960: Baby Boomers	18.56%
	1961–1979: Generation X	21.32%
	1980–1990: Generation Y	25.47%
	1991–2005: Generation Z	

Veterans or Pre-Boomers

This generation was born between the wars, and lived through the Second World War. Their values and beliefs are very different from their juniors. Work was considered a necessity; they have a strong loyalty to the company they work for and considered a job as for life. Thus they view work as an obligation and value hard work, sacrifice, duty before fun; they respect authority and adhere to rules. They have a preference for written communications and value the satisfaction of a job well done rather than tangible rewards.

Baby Boomers

The Baby Boomer Generation was born during or just after the war. They have seen the world dramatically change over their lifetime, through an industrial revolution, the rise of communication and technologies. In the

---

[26]Manpower (2007). Generation Y in the Workplace Australia; http://www.manpower. cz/images/GenerationYintheWorkplace.pdf.

[27]http://www.time.com/time/arts/article/0,8599,1731528,00.html#ixzz0sMc1zKDA.

[28]Manpower (2007). Generation Y in the Workplace Australia; http://www.manpower. cz/images/GenerationYintheWorkplace.pdf.

[29]US Census Bureau (2006). Facts for Features; http://www.census.gov/newsroom/ releases/archives/facts_for_features_special_editions/cb06-ffse01-2.html.

workplace the Baby Boomers are frequently described as workaholics and as team-players; they work efficiently, seek personal fulfilment and have a tendency to question authority. They prefer face-to-face communication and need to be valued and recognised.

Generation X

These are the children of the Baby Boomers, born in the late 1960s and 1970s; they are the one who mostly transformed the office as we know it today and our relation to work. They occupy today major senior management positions. This is a generation not always at ease in open offices. They are best motivated when allowed some flexibility on how to do a task and when the working environment is not rigidly rule-oriented.

Generation Y

Workers of the Generation Y, also known as the Millennial Generation, the 'Internet Generation', the 'iGeneration', or the 'MyPod Generation', are the generation broadly defined as those born between 1979 and 1999.[30] As more baby boomers retire, this substantially sized generation will become an increasingly vital segment of the workforce. In terms of work styles, professional expectations and career concerns, the Millennial's show some distinct preferences. Understanding these differences is fundamental to adapting motivational practices to correspond with their unique needs.

> *'With a BlackBerry in one hand, half-caf latte in the other and iPod-plugged earphones surgically attached to ears, they are ambitious, demanding and apparently born to rule.'*

Gen Ys should not be considered a single homogenous group; even within this group there have been significant developments between those under the age of 25 entering the workforce today, and those over 25. Those entering the workforce today have a distinct reliance on technology, believing they can work flexibly from anywhere and at anytime; they

---

[30]Patterson, B (2010). The A–Z of Generation Y (July 8, 2010) *The Sunday Herald*; http://www.heraldsun.com.au/news/sunday-heraldsun/a-z-of-generation-y/story-e6frf92; What Millenial workers want; how to attract and retain Gen Y employees, Robert Half International, http://www.hotjobsresources.com/pdfs/MillennialWorkers.pdf.

feel they should be evaluated on results, not on how, when or where they complete the task.[31]

A global study on Generation Y workers found differences between Asia and the rest of the world. The company brand is more important to Gen Ys in Asia than to Gen Ys elsewhere, favouring organisations with strong brand image. Lack of support and poor management are the main reasons for Asia-based Gen Ys leaving employment, whereas in the rest of the world the two most common reasons are that work is not motivating and to find better work-life balance. A number of common factors were found to be important to Generation Y all over the world: having the chance to learn and develop; the opportunity to do work that stimulates them; having a job aligned to their talents; having good managers who understand them; and being trusted, is central to keeping them motivated and engaged.[32]

Role in the workplace

Psychologists Ruth Kanfer and Phillip Ackerman have studied the effect of age-related changes on work motivation, and found that some job types are more likely than others to have a clear development track that may help keep people engaged in their careers over the long term. They suggest that there is a greater likelihood that professional workers with opportunities for role change and development may sustain higher levels of work motivation throughout the life course; in contrast, for service workers performing routinised tasks, the lack of opportunities for changes in work role may result in a slump in motivation and engagement in midlife and late adulthood.[33]

More than 85% of hiring managers and human resource executives said they feel that millennials have a stronger sense of entitlement than older workers. One dominant perception among managers today is that the millennials have much greater expectations. One survey identified their

---

[31] Manpower (2007). Generation Y in the Workplace Australia; http://www.manpower. cz/images/GenerationYintheWorkplace.pdf.

[32] TalentSmoothie (2008). Generation Y: Comparison between Asia and the rest of the world. http://www.talentsmoothie.com/wp-content/uploads/2009/12/Asia-GenY-highlights-2008.pdf.

[33] Kanfer, R and P Ackerman (2004). Aging, adult development, and work motivation. *Academy of Management Review*, 29(3), 440–458.

expectations as higher pay (74%); flexible work schedules (61%); a promotion within a year (56%); and more vacation or personal time (50%).[34]

Aside from managing higher expectations, retention is a greater challenge for the millennial generation than for previous generations. Millennials tend to have a more consumerist attitude towards their job and company, and can quickly decide to seek a better offer elsewhere if they find their needs inadequately satisfied. Money, benefits and growth were identified as the top three factors for moving jobs, according to one survey.[35]

Organisational Application

Many companies today are using customised approaches towards the different generations in the workplace. Xerox is using the slogan 'Express Yourself' as a way to describe its culture to new recruits. The hope is that the slogan will appeal to Gen Y's desire to develop solutions and change. Danone practices a strategy of recognition that is adapted to the different generations in the organisation.

David Cush, the President and CEO of Virgin American Airlines, emphasises the need to customise the approach towards the different generations in the organisation: 'With our younger workforce, there is a complete delta in how they expect to communicate. We need to build a multigenerational communication strategy to weave our diverse workforce together.'[36]

Lessons Learned

Understanding the needs of different generations is instrumental in developing motivational practices that are appropriate and effective. There is an increasing need for 'mass personalisation' in terms of autonomy, variety and flexibility.

---

[34]The trophy kids go to work, *Wall Street Journal* (2008); http://sec.online.wsj.com/article/SB122455219391652725.html.
[35]What Millenial workers want; how to attract and retain Gen Y employees, Robert Half International; http://www.hotjobsresources.com/pdfs/MillennialWorkers.pdf.
[36]IBM Global CEO Study (2010). *Capitalizing on Complexity Insights from the Global Chief Executive Officer Study*, p. 31.

4.3.2. Culture

Developed by Geert Hofstede (1970).

Overview

Culture is the collective programming of the mind that distinguishes the members of one group or category of people from another. Culture is learned, not inherited. It derives from one's social environment, not from one's genes. It is a collective phenomenon, because it is at least partly shared with people who live or lived within the same social environment, which is where it is learned.

Today all organisations have to understand the impact of a heterogeneous culture both inside and outside of the organisation. A globalised marketplace and higher levels of labour mobility mean that managing offices in different locations around the world or managing a multi-cultural workforce in the company's indigenous market means that cultural competence is an important issue for management. Cultural competence refers to an ability to interact effectively with people of different cultures. In essence, cultural competence and strong diversity management will help companies effectively draw upon talent, intellectual capital and motivate more employees.[37]

Coined by Hazel Hendersen in the 1970s, the iconic phrase 'Think Global, Act Local' is certainly valid for all managerial actions today. However, for many organisations, it is not only a case of thinking globally and acting locally, but simultaneously balancing multiple cultural needs within the same organisation.

Research by Hofstede and others provides us with valuable insight into understanding culture and cross-cultural differences. Geert Hofstede surveyed the work-related values of more than 116,000 IBM employees in 40 countries and defined culture as a 'programming of the mind,' which distinguishes one group of people from another.[38] Hofstede found that managers and employees differed on five value dimensions of national culture:

Power distance is the degree to which people in a country accept that power in institutions and organisations is distributed unequally. Power

---

[37] Cultural competence establishing a knowledge structure, *Business Week*; http://www.businessweek.com/adsections/diversity/diversecompet.htm.

[38] Hofstede, G (2005). *Cultures and Organizations, Software of the Mind.* New York: McGraw-Hill.

distance implies that in a hierarchical organisation, people in power will try to maintain their power, keeping power distance high. In high-power distance cultures, subordinates accept their status and respect formal hierarchical authority. Cultures low in power distance will have organisations where managers are willing to share authority.

Countries low in power distance include the United States, Australia, Great Britain and the Netherlands. Countries high in power distance include China, Mexico and West Africa.

Individualism-collectivism measures the degree to which people prefer to work as individuals rather than as group members. Cultures high in individualism respect personal achievement, autonomy and innovation. On the other hand, cultures high on collectivism emphasise group harmony, social order, loyalty and personal relationships. Individual contributions are not valued if they work against group goals or interests. In order to maintain harmony in a collectivist culture, it is often necessary to be conservative and cautious. Power distance and individual collectivism have become the primary factors that differentiate cultures and have received the most attention from researchers.

Masculinity-femininity is the degree to which perceived typical male attributes (e.g. assertiveness, success and competition) prevail over perceived typically feminine attributes (e.g. sensitivity and concern for others). Cultures high in masculinity are more likely to be male-dominated, especially in management, whereas in cultures that are defined as feminine it is more likely to find women in managerial and professional positions.

Uncertainty Avoidance Index deals with a society's tolerance for uncertainty and ambiguity; it ultimately refers to man's search for Truth. It indicates to what extent a culture programs its members to feel either uncomfortable or comfortable in unstructured situations. Uncertainty avoiding cultures try to minimise the possibility of unstructured situations by strict laws and rules, safety and security measures and on the philosophical and religious level by a belief in absolute Truth. Uncertainty accepting cultures are more tolerant of opinions different from what they are used to; they try to have as few rules as possible, and on the philosophical and religious level they are relativist and allow many schools of thought to exist side by side.

Long-term orientation versus short-term orientation: This fifth dimension was found in a study among students in 23 countries around the world, using a questionnaire designed by a Chinese scholar. Values associated with long-term orientation are thrift and perseverance; values associated with short-term orientation are respect for tradition, fulfilling social obligations and protecting one's 'face'.

Organisational Application

Sodexo

Sodexo have been awarded one of the top honours for diversity; present in over 80 countries, Sodexo are perfectly placed to understand the challenges of cultural differences. The Chief Executive believes that one of the most important qualities for a company embracing cultural diversity is having the humility to say 'I don't know', trying to put yourself in another's shoes is not possible without making a big effort. That is why Sodexo is trying to develop this empathetic attitude in the organisation by training people to develop an awareness.[39]

Microsoft

In the Microsoft European headquarters in Dublin, understanding the needs of the diverse market is an integral part of company success; a diverse employee makeup plays a key role in business strategy. In turn, the creation of an inclusive environment is critical to managing a multicultural workforce. As one employee states: 'at any given day you can hear about five different languages in the cafeteria. It's such a great feeling to be surrounded by so many people from various places, with varying experiences and cultures—and who all have strong mutual respect. It's one of the things that I admire most about Microsoft.'[40]

Lessons Learned

All organisations have to understand the impact of a heterogeneous culture both inside and outside of the organisation. A globalised market-place and higher levels of labour mobility mean that managing offices in different locations around the world or managing a multi-cultural workforce in the company's indigenous market means that cultural competence is an important issue for management. Cultural competence refers to an ability to interact effectively with people of different cultures.

---

[39]The Top 50 Companies for Diversity, *Diversity Inc Magazine* (June 2010); http://www.diversityinc.com/pages/DI_50_2011.shtml.
[40]Microsoft Careers Ireland; https://careers.microsoft.com/careers/EN/IE/ProfileIna.aspx.

In essence, cultural competence and strong diversity management will help companies effectively draw upon talent, intellectual capital and motivate employees more effectively.

4.3.3. *Personality*

Developed by P.T. Costa and R.R. McCrae (1992); J.M. Digman (1990); M.T. Russell and D. Karol (1994).

Overview

Personality has been defined as 'an individual's characteristic patterns of thought, emotion, and behavior, together with the psychological mechanisms — hidden or not — behind those patterns[41]'.

Personality dimensions, in combination with situational moderators like success, failure, pressure and incentives, affect both motivation and performance. They operate dynamically to prioritise which goals would guide the specific implementation of which tasks and behaviours.

Research in psychology has given rise to a model with five dimensions that has become a reference for personality psychologists. The Five-Factor Model of personality[42] also referred to as the Big Five model[43] or the Global Factors of Personality[44] was discovered and defined by several independent sets of researchers who identified generally the same five dimensions. Each of these broad traits has many specific facets or subcomponents that correlate together.

The Big Five factors and their constituent traits can be summarised as follows:

Extraversion represents individual differences in the tendency to seek stimulation in the company of others: warm, affectionate, sociable, talkative, assertive, energetic, excitement-seeking, experiencing positive emotions.

---

[41]Funder, DC (2001). *The Personality Puzzle*, 2nd Ed. New York: Norton.

[42]Costa, PT, Jr. and RR McCrae (1992). *Revised NEO Personality Inventory (NEO-PI-R) and NEO Five-Factor Inventory (NEO-FFI) Manual.* Odessa, FL: Psychological Assessment Resources.

[43]Digman, JM (1990). Personality structure: Emergence of the five-factor model. *Annual Review of Psychology*, 41, 417–440.

[44]Russell, MT and D Karol (1994). *16PF Fifth Edition Administrator's Manual.* Champaign, IL: Institute for Personality & Ability Testing.

Agreeableness represents individual differences in the tendency to be compassionate and cooperative towards others: friendly, altruistic, honest and trusting, well-intentioned, kind, sincere.

Conscientiousness represents individual differences in the tendency to place a high value on competence and efficacy, innate capabilities and the acquisition of skills — self-disciplined, efficient, trustworthy and reliable, morally upright and principled, ambitious, organised.

Neuroticism represents individual differences in the tendency to experience emotional instability: distress, moodiness, irritability, sadness, anger, anxiety or depression.

Openness to experience represents individual differences in the tendency to imagine and create — inventive, curious, aesthetically-sensitive, daring, fully experiencing emotions, real-life and intimacy.

The Five Factor Model is a purely descriptive model of personality, but psychologists have developed a number of theories to account for the Big Five. Research has developed in the cognitive field on that topic. It suggests that personality traits are the consequences of adaptive strategies that result from a set of individual goals, beliefs, intentions and resources.[45] For example, the trait 'helpful' can be broken down into the goal to help others, beliefs about the value of helping others and whether others deserve help, the intention to help and the resources to do so.[46] Recent findings in neuroscience and temperament provide evidence that there is a biological basis for some of the dimensions of personalities listed in the Five-Factor Model of personality; this link is the subject of much ongoing research.

Studies suggest that personality is largely influenced by the social-cultural environment; hence, looking at collective specificities (nationality or generation for instance) may contribute to the understanding of personality traits.

Role in the organisation today

Motivation and personality go hand in hand: different people and personalities are motivated by different drives.

---

[45]Read, SJ and LC Miller (1998). On the dynamic construction of meaning: An interactive activation and competition model of social perception. In *Connectionist Models of Social Reasoning and Behavior*, SJ Read and LC Miller (eds.), pp. 27–68. Mahwah, NJ: Erlbaum.

[46]Zachary, W, J-C LeMentec, L Miller, S Read and G Thomas-Meyers. Steps toward a Personality-based Architecture for Cognition. Proceedings of the Annual Conference on Behavioral Representation in Modeling and Simulation, Los Angeles, CA/NA.

Taking into account people's personalities is especially important in two work situations: when it comes to finding the right fit between a person and a function or mission, and when it comes to leveraging individual performance. The challenge for both recruiters and managers is to assess the individual and the circumstances and set the motivational framework accordingly (motivational levers, expectations and goals, recognition and reinforcement and so on): What are the worker's preferences and competencies? Is there a propensity for challenge? How are awards and recognition perceived? Does he or she have confidence in his or her abilities? What are his or her personal needs, goals and expectations?

Numerous personality assessment tools have been created to help organisations assess and understand personality differences.

Lessons Learned

Personality dimensions, in combination with situational moderators like success, failure, pressure and incentives, affect motivation and performance. They dynamically operate to prioritise which goals would guide the specific implementation of which tasks and behaviours.

Therefore uniform motivational practices will not yield a uniform quality of performance; different personality types respond differently to the same motivational opportunities. Organisations need to understand individual differences, values and needs and adapt motivational techniques according to the person.

4.4.   Summary of the Architecture of Motivation at Work

4.4.1.   *A Supportive Framework*

Management Styles Douglas McGregor, 1960	Management styles have a profound impact on employee motivation, morale and the success of the organisation. Managers today must balance the needs of the organisation with the needs of the employee in order for sustainable growth to occur in the organisation. McGregor draws attention to the benefits of positive management styles that encourage responsibility and growth through the development of his Theory Y of management. Theory

(Continued)

(Continued)

	Y assumes that the potential for motivation and development, the capacity to assume responsibility and the willingness to direct behaviour towards organisational goals are present in all people.
Goal-setting Edwin Locke and Gary Latham, 1981	Goal-setting is one of the most effective and widely used methods of guiding motivation in the organisation today. Goals influence performance by directing attention, regulating effort, increasing persistence and encouraging goal attainment strategies. A goal serves as a motivator because it causes people to compare their present capacity to perform with that required to succeed at the goal and thereby stimulating an increase in performance, that is, goals serve as a yardstick for improvement in performance.
Fairness J.S. Adams, 1967 and Jerald Greenberg, 1987	Maintaining an equitable and transparent system of compensation and reward and organisational procedures is important for establishing perceptions of fairness in the organisation which is an important factor of employee satisfaction. Although it is common to have different deviations among different levels of employees, the system for attaining compensation raises must be equitable and transparent in order to create a motivation to strive for pay increases through increased effort.

4.4.2. Considering Individual Specificities

Stage of Life	Understanding the needs of different generations is instrumental in developing motivational practices that are appropriate and effective. There is an increasing need for 'mass personalisation' in terms of autonomy, variety and flexibility.
Culture Geert Hofstede, 1970	All organisations have to understand the impact of a heterogeneous culture both inside and outside of the organisation. A globalised marketplace and higher

(Continued)

(Continued)

	levels of labour mobility mean that managing offices in different locations around the world or managing a multi-cultural workforce in the company's indigenous market means that cultural competence is an important issue for management. Cultural competence refers to an ability to interact effectively with people of different cultures. In essence, cultural competence and strong diversity management will help companies draw upon talent, intellectual capital and motivate employees effectively.
Personality	Personality has been defined as 'an individual's characteristic patterns of thought, emotion, and behavior, together with the psychological mechanisms — hidden or not — behind those patterns[47]'.
P.T. Costa and R.R. McCrae, 1992; J.M. Digman, 1990; M.T. Russell, D. Karol, 1994	Thus, while an individual's values are likely to influence behaviour in the workplace, personality is likely to be more direct measure of actual behaviour. Uniform motivational practices will not yield a uniform quality of performance; different personality types respond differently to the same motivational opportunities. Thus, one of the key lessons for the organisation today is the need to understand individual differences, values and needs and to adapt motivational techniques according to the person.

---

[47]Funder, DC (2001). *The Personality Puzzle*, 2nd Ed. New York: Norton.

PART 2

BUILDING MOTIVATION AT WORK IN THE CONTEMPORARY ENVIRONMENT

This section on 'Building Motivation at Work' explores how motivation is understood and put into practice by organisations today. According to the unique needs of the company and the individual needs of the employees, successful companies adapt motivational practices to drive the success of the organisation. Based on the reconciliation of the theoretical foundations of motivation, and the lessons learned from successful contemporary organisations, a motivation spectrum has been developed that demonstrates the many levers which contribute to the creation of sustainable motivation. This motivation spectrum is designed to foster motivation and bring out the best of employees for individual and organisational success.

The Challenges for the 21st Century Organisation

Today's economy is characterised by several defining forces: the rise in knowledge intensity of economic activities, the globalisation of manufacturing and services and the predominance of services as a source of economic growth. Cutting across all of these factors is the decisive role people play in all of these organisational activities. In this 'people-based economy', the determinants of business success — innovation, creativity, execution, and service — are dependent on the behaviour and motivation of the people in the organisation.[1]

In this dynamic economy where firms are battling for the same market space organisations have to continually reinvent who they are and what they do in both large and small ways. The ability to innovate and to adapt creatively to the competitive environment can only be achieved through the people in the organisation.[2] Thus, managing the human asset has become an increasingly strategic factor in leveraging this asset to achieve business success.

Over time, the firms that have built their organisations with motivated, engaged and connected people have proven to be the most successful at reinventing themselves to achieve sustainable performance and success. Knowledge in the organisation is now being regarded as a key resource, possessing and producing value, and driving innovation. According to the OECD, the 'knowledge distribution power' of the organisation is a major determinant of organisational prosperity.[3] Central to this dissemination of knowledge is the collaboration of people within the organisation, their shared vision, and their capacity to work together to innovate.

Vestiges of industrial era management methods where the people in the organisation are treated as 'factors of production' remain apparent in today's working world.[4] The competitive struggle for market share has reduced the majority of companies into '*short-term management*' structures that enable them to quickly dispose of or add members of staff; this commodity-style management has reduced the sense of community, belonging and engagement in organisations. People no longer feel loyal towards the organisation, because the organisation is not loyal to them; their sense of value and security has diminished.[5] And yet, acceptable standards of working conditions have changed dramatically over the past 30 years. There is a greater focus today on the quality of life of the people in

---

[1] Won-joo, Yun and F Mulhern (2009). Leadership and the performance of people in organizations: Enriching employees and connecting people. *Forum for People Performance Management and Measurement Publication*, November 2009.

[2] McDonough, EF, MH Zach, H ErLin and I Berdrow (2008). Integrating innovation style and knowledge into strategy. *MIT Sloan Management Review*, 50(1), October.

[3] OECD (1996). *The Knowledge-Based Economy*. Paris: OECD.

[4] Won-joo, Yun and F Mulhern (2009). Leadership and the performance of people in organizations: Enriching employees and connecting people. *Forum for People Performance Management and Measurement Publication*, November 2009.

[5] Minztberg, H (2009). Rebuilding companies as communities. *Harvard Business Review*, July–August 2009.

the organisation. The time is past when employees, grateful to have any job at all, will tolerate adverse working conditions or a cantankerous manager in exchange for a paycheck. People today are fundamentally concerned about physical, psychological and social aspects of their lives in ways that span both workplace and private life.[6]

In contrast to an industrial era approach to leadership, a people-centric approach is more appropriate for the emerging knowledge and services economy. The importance today of collaboration amongst people in the organisation has been highlighted by many studies. Frank Mulhern of Northwestern University refers to this as the 'human value connection'. This represents what Mulhern refers to as a 'flow of performance'; organisations succeed because information and actions flow from person to person. Henry Minztberg too has asserted the need for companies to foster a sense of 'communityship' within the organisation, for companies to rebuild themselves into places of engagement, where people are committed to one another and their organisation. Minztberg advocates a move away from the individualist behavior towards practices that promote trust, engagement and spontaneous collaboration aimed at sustainability.[7]

This emphasis on collective collaboration, rather than a set of individual, disparate attitudes is increasingly being identified as a key determinant of innovation in the organisation. 'The need to innovate quickly is becoming more important to business', confirms Robert Whiteside, Google head of enterprise UK, Ireland and Benelux. A study conducted in 2010 finds an 81% positive correlation between collaboration and innovation across all markets. In the UK, employees who are given the opportunity to collaborate at work are nearly twice as likely to have contributed new ideas to their companies. This sets the priority for the management of people in the 21st century economy. Management will need to ensure employees are motivated to collaborate and innovate, and to foster a sense of corporate community.[8]

Fostering this sense of 'communityship', according to Minztberg, means 'caring about our work, our colleagues, and our place in the world', and in

[6]Won-joo, Yun and F Mulhern (2009). Leadership and the performance of people in organizations: Enriching employees and connecting people. *Forum for People Performance Management and Measurement Publication*, November 2009.

[7]Minztberg, H (2009). Rebuilding companies as communities. *Harvard Business Review*, July–August 2009.

[8]Harrington, S (2010). Google research heralds arrival of the new human systems director, HR Magazine, 10 June 2010; http://www.hrmagazine.co.uk/news/1009061/ Exclusive-Google-research-heralds-arrival-human-systems-director/.

turn being inspired by this caring. A case in point is that of Southwest Airlines, the airline company that has never resorted to a furlough to bring about a short-term resolution to a difficult operating environment. The result of this is a body of employees that trust the organisation and are happy to reciprocate with passionate service and contribute innovative solutions to help the company to prosper.

Collaboration and a community spirit can only be achieved by valuing the people in the organisation and fostering a sense of trust amongst people and management. The axiom that organisations are only as good as their people rings true today with companies increasingly proving that the optimal way to profitability is by putting people first.

Chapter 5

LEVERAGING MOTIVATION
IN THE ORGANISATION TODAY

Numerous factors operate in tandem to create and sustain a person's happiness, satisfaction and engagement at work. Motivation is not something that can be hastily introduced with a set of 'quick-fix' measures. In today's most successful organisations, motivation has been built with an entire spectrum of motivational levers to create value for both the employer and the employee.

We know that people are not motivated singularly by a large salary, an attractive benefits package or because of a likeable manager. Just as humans are complex, and seek purpose and meaning from life, motivating people to put forth their best effort at work is equally complex.

Numerous factors operate in tandem to create and sustain a person's happiness, satisfaction and engagement at work. Many of these factors are not easily decipherable; only through actively speaking and listening to employees can the unique desires and aspirations of each employee be discerned. Equally, this two-way communication is indispensable for ensuring employees can work collaboratively towards the common objectives and successful performance of the organisation, the *raison d'être* for business. Moreover, motivation is an unstable process; the determinants of employee motivation can change and evolve over time. The employee who walks through the door of the company on his first day is likely to be motivated by an entirely new set of factors 20 years later.

The theoretical foundations of motivation in Part 1 allow us to understand humans — our physiological and psychological needs and desires, our behaviours, and the processes that drive us to work in a certain way. Part 2 aims to translate the understanding of human motivation into actionable knowledge. *Building Motivation at Work* is an exploration of how these understandings are put in to practice by organisations today. By analysing the best practices of successful organisations we discovered that each company has a unique recipe for creating and sustaining motivation, consistent with the needs of the company, the organisational constraints, and according to the unique needs, desires and aspirations of the employees. Despite the heterogeneity of company approaches, our analysis revealed a set of similarities in the practices of these successful companies, which enabled us to synthesize the results in a model of motivation. Based on these findings, we have designed a new model of motivation at work: the *Motivation Spectrum*. This model reconciles the theoretical foundations, in order to understand the logic behind the action, as well as with organisational examples and studies, to allow us to see the effect of the different motivation drivers in action. All of these companies approach motivation as a combined set of intrinsic and extrinsic factors, with a collective and an individual approach. Above all, these companies respect and value the unique knowledge, contributions and potential of their employees and treat them as the key asset of organisational success.

5.1. The Motivation Spectrum

Motivation is not something that can be hastily introduced in the organisation with a set of 'quick-fix' measures. In today's most successful organisations, motivation has been comprehensively built into daily management practices to create a balanced and positive relationship between the employer and the employee, thereby creating a reciprocal value for both. The Motivation Spectrum is a set of universal drivers that can be adapted according to the needs of the organisation and the unique needs of its people to foster motivation in the workplace.

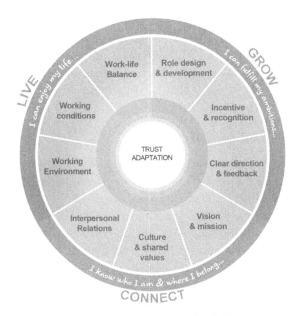

ESSEC ISIS/ Sodexo Institute for Quality of Daily Life 2010

5.2. The Preconditions for Sustainable Motivation

5.2.1. *Trust: Creating a Reciprocal Relationship Transparency, Accountability, Fairness*

> *'No company, nonprofit, or government agency can prevent a major catastrophe, but you can build an organization that is battle-ready, that has high morale, that knows how to behave, that trusts itself and where people trust one another.'*
>
> *Peter Drucker*

Creating strong reciprocal relationships between the leaders and the employees should be first underpinned by several leadership 'prerequisites' conducive to creating a relationship of trust and mutual value. As Peter Drucker, the renowned management guru, states, 'organisations are no longer built on force. They are increasingly built on trust'.[1]

---

[1] Drucker, P (1982). *Management Challenges for the 21st Century*. Oxford: Elsevier.

As Louis Barnes explained, trust creates a sense of reciprocity; people respond in kind to the way how they are treated. Yet, trust is a difficult value to foster at the workplace, particularly in difficult economic times when fears of layoff are a constant threat to the employee–employer relationships.

Zoom on ... Organisational Trust

Louis Barnes, a professor at Harvard Business School, studied organisational trust and found it linked to the theory of reciprocity; the idea that people respond in kind to the way that they are treated.

Peter Drucker emphasised that 'trust means that you know what to expect of people. Trust is mutual understanding'. Trustworthiness means establishing a code of conduct and being consistent in the application of these principles so that employees can see that leaders do what they say and 'walk the talk'. Yet, polls in recent years by Watson Wyatt, BlessingWhite, and others have found that fewer than half of all workers trust what senior management is telling them.[2]

Each year, the Great Place to Work Institute surveys tens of thousands of employees through its 'Trust Index' and then extols those companies that offer extraordinary environments of 'credibility, respect, fairness, pride, and camaraderie'.[3]

Leveraging sustainable motivation at work is supported by strong organisational values of fairness, transparency and accountability. The organisations benchmarked in the study made the values of fairness, transparency and accountability a central pillar in its relationship with the people in the organisation.

Creating a relationship of trust leads to a greater degree of accountability on the part of the employees; people feel like owners of the business and know that they play an important role in the success of the organisation. In Southwest Airlines, employees have always been treated as owners. Aside from a profit-sharing plan, employees are reminded that they alone

---

[2]Trust: Effective managers make it a priority (16 October 2009) in *BusinessWeek*; http://www.businessweek.com/managing/content/oct2009/ca20091019_333718.htm.
[3]Trust: Effective managers make it a priority (16 October 2009) in *BusinessWeek*; http://www.businessweek.com/managing/content/oct2009/ca20091019_333718.htm.

carry the torch for the company values and they are accountable for their actions, which have an influence on the company's success. As Colleen Barrett, President Emeritus of Southwest Airlines asserts, 'as employees you are owners of this airline . . . we encourage people to as long as they hold themselves accountable first, to then hold others accountable. As long as they do it in a respectful way.'

Spotlight on the Theory: Theory X and Theory Y

Douglas McGregor (1960s)

McGregor draws attention to the benefits of positive leadership styles that encourage responsibility and individual growth in order for sustainable motivation to occur in the organisation.

McGregor examined the effects of management styles on employee motivation. He proposed two opposing motivational models called Theory X and Theory Y.

Theory X was based on the assumption that employees dislike work and seek to avoid responsibility; people work only for money and security. Therefore to achieve organisational objectives, a business would need to impose a management system of coercion, control and punishment.

Theory Y was based on the assumption that employees are creative, seek responsibility and can exercise self direction. The challenge for management is therefore to design jobs to expand opportunities and thus enable employees to grow and give more of their innate potential to the business.

McGregor himself asserted that the assumptions of Theory X are negative and not sustainable. The X model has been proven to be counter-effective in most modern practice. On the contrary, **McGregor concluded that managers who involve their employees in decision making and present more challenges encourage effective performance**. Theory Y recommended what Herzberg in 1964 called 'job enrichment' and Peters in 1982 and 1985 called 'empowerment.'

In HCL too, accountability is promoted from the bottom-up. The 'Employee First, Customer Second' philosophy in HCL places the needs of the employees before the needs of the customers. The aim is to create a unique employee organisation, drive an inverted organisational structure, create transparency and accountability within the organisation and encourage a value-driven culture. The company's CEO Vineet Nayar considers this instrumental for the success of the business: 'An employee is not a tool in the hands of a CEO, but a CEO is a tool in the hands of the employee — if you do that you will unleash the energy of 50,000 employees in the world which is unbeatable.'[4]

Zoom on... Fairness

Sodexo's practices to promote gender equality in the workplace.[5]

Sodexo is a French multinational corporation in quality-of-life services. Sodexo employs approximately 355,000 persons, representing 130 nationalities and is present in 30,600 locations in 80 countries. Sodexo has a strong commitment to diversity and inclusion with four priorities: gender, people with disabilities, generations and ethnic minorities. The main priority is on gender and Sodexo has embarked on a very deliberate strategy to increase the representation of women in middle and higher management, driven by the CEO Michel Landel, who says that '... diversity and inclusion... is a business imperative that drives the company's ability to attract and develop the best talent, create an engaged workforce, and deliver quality of life solutions to the diverse clients and customers.'

Organisational trust can be difficult to foster, unless it is lived by all members of the organisation, from the leader down to the last employee. As Peter Drucker states, 'The leaders who work most effectively... never say 'I', and that's not because they have trained themselves not to say 'I'. They don't think 'I'. They think 'we'; they think 'team'... '.[6] It is by creating a two-way dialogue with employees, looking after their well-being and treating them with respect and fairness, that the values of trust can be cultivated in the organisation.

---

[4]Insead: In search of blue oceans: HCL Technologies; http://knowledge.insead.edu/BOSHCLTechnologies080509.cfm.

[5]'Study on non-legislative initiatives for companies to promote gender equality at the workplace', conducted in March 2010 by the Austrian Institute for SME Research on behalf of the European Commission, Directorate-General for Employment, Social Affairs and Equal Opportunities.

[6]Trust: Effective managers make it a priority (16 October 2009) in *Business Week*; http://www.businessweek.com/managing/content/oct2009/ca20091019_333718.htm.

5.2.2.   *Adapt: The Importance of Personalisation*

'The personal touch always makes the reward seem sweeter.'

Leah Shepherd

Organisations today are realising the importance of personal touch when dealing with employees. Individualised recognition and offering a degree of personalisation and choice for such things as incentives, benefits or working schedule has a greater value than simply offering a one-size-fits-all strategy. As Leah Shepherd notes, 'the personal touch always makes the reward seem sweeter'.[7]

According to research by Buckingham (2005) and the results of an extensive Gallup survey, there is one quality that sets truly great managers apart from the rest: 'They discover what is unique about each person and then capitalise on it'. Great managers know and value the unique abilities and the idiosyncrasies of their employees. Managers will succeed only when they can identify and deploy the differences among people, challenging each employee to excel in his or her own way.[8]

Buckingham also revealed the importance of tailoring motivation to the individual. Knowing the person can help not only to identify their goals and aspirations, and how they are motivated, but also to trigger good performance. Recognition, for instance, can be practiced in many different ways: publicly, privately, via a customer, etc. A manager must be able to match the employee to the audience he values most. One employee's audience might be his peers; the best way to praise him would be to stand him up in front of his co-workers and publicly celebrate his achievement. Another's favourite audience might be the manager; the most powerful recognition would be a one-on-one conversation where the manager tells him privately why he is such a valuable member of the team.[9]

According to Frank Mulhern, there are two key processes for effective people-centered management today: 'employee insight', understanding what motivates and satisfies employees and 'employee segmentation', the use of

---

[7]Shepherd, L (2010). Special Report on Rewards & Recognition: Getting Personal (September). *Workplace Management*; http://www.workforce.com/section/benefits-compensation/feature/special-report-rewards-recognition-getting-personal/index.html.

[8]Buckingham, M (2005). What great managers do. *Harvard Business Review*, March, 70–79.

[9]Buckingham, M (2005). What great managers do. *Harvard Business Review*, March, 70–79.

customised offerings (communications, benefit programs) that are relevant to different types of people based on an understanding of their personal concerns.[10]

Instead of striving for sameness, companies should look for ways to offer their workers choices about everything from their work hours to their pay structure to how they attend training sessions. Employees who feel their company is trying to support them personally are much more likely to be engaged in their work and do a better job. 'Everything people do today in their consumer lives, from a very early age, is customised', says David Smith, author of *Workforce of One: Revolutionizing Talent Management Through Customization*. This practice, he contends, has led to a growing sense that people should also be able to shape their work lives to meet their preferences.[11] As part of his research, Smith surveyed employees to find out what made them happy and what did not. The organisations where workers felt personally supported shared four features: they segmented the workforce creatively; they extended a cafeteria model of health benefits to offer modular choices in other areas; they defined broad and simple rules about work that could be applied in different ways; and, in some cases, they let employees define the parameters of what they need.

It is important to note the value of a regular two-way communication process to listen and communicate frequently with employees, both individually and collectively, in order to understand what is important to them. Knowing an employee's needs, desires and aspirations will tell managers what motivates them: are they looking for career advancement or more challenging work? Do they need more appreciation for their work? Are there things that are causing dissatisfaction, such as the working schedule, which could be altered to improve the employee's satisfaction with the working environment? HCL, an Indian PC manufacturer and IT services provider, has put in place an Internet forum called 'U&I' that allows employees to interact directly with the CEO. The CEO himself spends time answering employee questions and concerns.[12]

---

[10]Won-joo, Yun and F Mulhern (2009). Leadership and the performance of people in organizations: Enriching employees and connecting people. *Forum for People Performance Management and Measurement Publication*, November.

[11]Smith, D and S Cantrall (2010). Workforce of one: Revolutionizing talent management through customization. *Harvard Business Press*; http://www.cfo.com/article.cfm/14506183/c_14507235?f=home_todayinfinance.

[12]Nayar V (2010). *Employees First, Customers Second*. Boston: Harvard Business Press.

Table 5.1   Important factors to attract people to a job.

The Emerging Economies	Brazil	China	India	The Mature Economies	Germany	U.K.	U.S.
Career advancement	1	1	1	Competitive salary	*	1	1
Competitive salary	2	*	*	Convenient work location	2	2	*
Challenging work	3	*	3	Sufficient vacation	*	3	2
Learning and development opportunities	*	2	2	Challenging work	1	*	*
Competitive benefits	*	3	*	Flexible schedule	3	*	*
				Competitive health care	*	*	3

Source: Insights from the 2010 Global Workforce Study, Towers Perrin.

Table 5.1 itemises the most important factors for attracting people to a job across different countries. It highlights the differences across cultures, but these factors can change over the course of an employee lifetime, or due to changes in circumstances. Thus, the implementation of an open dialogue with employees is key to understanding what motivates and satisfies employees over time.

5.3.   The Levers of Motivation

Leveraging motivation at work is driven by three fundamental needs: the need to *live*, *grow* and *connect*. We are motivated by the need to live a full and healthy life; the desire to grow, to challenge ourselves and to develop professionally; and the need to somehow connect with people and the organisation in which we work to find a sense of meaning and belonging in our daily lives. In order for people to be motivated to reach their full potential at work, to be content in their role and their environs, an organisation should seek to provide the means to satisfy these needs.

According to Abraham Maslow's theory of motivation, human life can reach its greatest potential, known as the concept of *self-actualisation*, if people have the means to fulfil their innate needs. What drives us, or motivates us, in life as in work, are the needs that we strive to satisfy; as Maslow once said, 'the human being is simultaneously that which he is and that which he yearns to be'.[13] Maslow was one of the first theorists to link human motivation with well-being and positive psychology.[14]

Employee performance and motivation today is influenced by the ability to balance the demands and objectives of the organisation, with the needs, aspirations and concerns of the employee. These needs and concerns are not restricted to the 'nine-to-five' hours of the employee; the evolution of the working environment means that longer, more stressful commutes, greater demands on a person's time and '24/7' connectivity have become commonplace. The longer-term effects of such a lifestyle cannot be ignored by the organisation and employee needs should be holistically managed in order to stimulate positive motivation for the organisation.

---

[13] Maslow, A (1962). *Toward a Psychology of Being*. New York: Van Nostrand.
[14] Lambert, C (2007). The science of happiness (January–February 2007). *Harvard Magazine*, p. 26.

5.4. Live: I Can Enjoy My Life . . . .

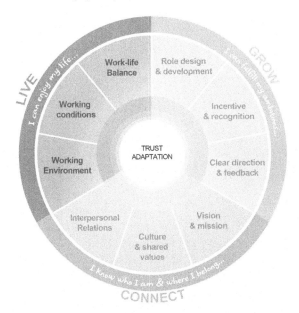

Work is primarily a means to earn a living, a source of income with which to finance our need for food and shelter, to raise a family and to feel safe. Thus, the drive to *live* is necessarily a fundamental need that must be met by the organisation. The physical environment, the working conditions and the resources provided by the organisation that enable an employee to carry out the requirement of the employment have an important impact on physical and psychological well-being. What we experience in our daily lives at work inevitably has an impact on our psychological and emotional well-being. The rise in stress-related illness in contemporary society highlights the importance of physical and psychological well-being in relation to employee motivation and performance. We look at the needs of employees that are essential to motivation at work through the levers of working environment, working conditions and work-life balance.

5.4.1.   *Working Environment*

'We shape our buildings: thereafter they shape us.'

Winston Churchill

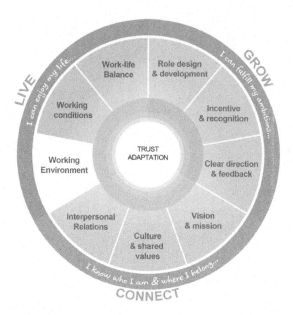

The working environment plays an integral role in creating conditions propitious for motivation and enabling a high level of service and quality of work. A good working environment is safe and comfortable, it facilitates professional life by providing proper resources and taking care of people's daily needs, it promotes team working and conviviality; this can foster positive attitudes towards work and the organisation helping to sustain the right attitude for motivated behavior.

Working Environment, Definition:

The working environment refers to the physical workplace, the availability of relevant technological or communication resources, workplace security and safety, the cleanliness and ergonomics of the workspace, the level of noise and the lighting, the availability of canteen facilities, proximity to public transport, shops and facilities; the codes of behavior that define the workplace; the factors that make work physically possible, safe, pleasant and convivial.

The physical working environment

We spend a great deal of our time at work, the four walls where we spend the greater part of our waking hours necessarily affects our well-being, our attitudes towards work, and our perception of company culture. A pleasant and safe working environment is a primary condition for fostering motivation at work; as one *Wall Street Journal* reporter remarks, 'offering flexible work hours, generous stock options, and an anything-goes dress code isn't enough, it turns out, if the office is dingy, dull or developer-conceived rather than custom-made'.[15]

Health and safety

All businesses must ensure their workplace — whether it is a factory, office or shop — meets minimum health and safety standards: safe use of machinery, tools and IT equipment; assessment of risks, health and safety notices and signs in the workplace; fire safety standards and first aid equipment. There are basic standards of comfort and sanitation that every workplace should meet: clean toilets and sanitation facilities, sufficient space and ventilation for people to work comfortably, temperature of the building and water supply.

> *'Offering flexible hours, generous stock-options, and an anything-goes dress code isn't enough, it turns out, if the office is dingy, dull or developer-conceived rather than custom-made.'*
>
> Kevin Helliker

Ergonomics and space design

The typical office worker spends more hours a week in their chair than most of them spend in their beds. The design and the ergonomics of the workspace inevitably impact the worker: the colour the office is painted; the furniture type and quality; the presence or absence of exterior view and light; and the ability to hear or see fellow workers. A recent before-and-after study of major upgrades in furniture at a large insurance company headquarters showed a 53% increase in productivity and a 14% drop in absenteeism after the new furniture was installed.[16]

---

[15] Helliker, K (1998). Can trees and jogging trails lure techies to Kansas? (21 October 1998). *Wall Street Journal*, P. B1.
[16] Wiedenkeller, K (2010). SVP, Human Resources, AMC Entertainment in 'Some like it hot? Work environments impact productivity' (4 May 2010). *Film Journal International*;

Spotlight on the Theory: Two-factor Theory

Frederick Herzberg (1959)

Providing a good working environment

Herzberg distinguished between two types of needs: hygiene and motivators. He identified the working environment as hygiene factor of motivation; this means that if the employee is dissatisfied with the quality of the working environment, it can quickly lead to dissatisfaction and demotivation. Yet, according to Herzberg, the working environment, once deemed satisfactory by the employee, does not have a strong impact on motivation. This is where the motivators play a role.

Motivator factors relate directly to the job itself; they refer to intrinsic factors in the job such as responsibilities, opportunities for promotion, autonomy, work challenge, task meaningfulness and interest; these factors correspond with the higher-order needs in Maslow's hierarchy.[17] It is necessary to satisfy both physical (hygiene) and psychological (motivator) needs concurrently to ensure sustained motivation, employee satisfaction and performance.

Open plan offices have many advantages such as ease of communication and access, closer contact with fellow workers, closer supervision and monitoring, but there may be noise-related disadvantages and it often creates an environment in which people are perceptually over-stimulated.[18] Researchers have found that individual performance increases by 25% when employees use an ergonomically designed workstation.[19] A survey by Microsoft corroborates this view with 90% of those surveyed saying that the design setup of their workstation directly affects their ability to be most productive at work.[20]

---

http://www.filmjournal.com/filmjournal/content_display/columns-and-blogs/the-people-factor/e3i7b2c50df9c8f86ff8be25b86bc20bd72.

[17] Amabile, TM (1993). Motivational synergy: Toward new conceptualizations of intrinsic and extrinsic motivation in the workplace. *Human Resource Management Review*, 3(3), 185–201.

[18] Loewen, LJ and P Suedfeld (1992). Cognitive and arousal effects of masking office noise. *Environment and Behavior Journal*, 24(3), 381–395.

[19] Pheasant, S (1991). *Ergonomics, Work and Health*. London: Macmillan Publishing.

[20] Microsoft (2004). Nine out of ten employees link workplace design to their productivity, June; http://www.microsoft.com/presspass/press/2004/jun04/06-28Work placeDesignPR.mspx.

Building organisation

The location and organisation of a building has an impact on attracting people to work in the organisation as well as having a real impact on people's daily lives at work. A building located in the centre of a city may be preferable as a location that people can get to quickly; yet there may be a compromise on space. Similarly the design of the work area is an important issue. An open-plan office may be suitable for IT workers who would have a lot of mobility in their jobs; yet, it may not work for another type of worker. 'The nature of a person's work should dictate decisions about space. Form should follow function'.[21]

Workplace design

While there is a minimum standard of comfort to be met to facilitate performance; the working environment can also be leveraged as a tool to foster positive attitudes that facilitate interaction and make employees feel valued. Substantial evidence exists today to suggest that the working environment can be leveraged to positively impact employee morale, motivation and performance. In essence, it plays an influential role in shaping our desire to work in a particular organisation and in moulding our motivation at work.

Zoom on ... Workplace Design and Productivity

The 2006 U.S. Workplace Survey revealed that the workplace is also a significant factor to U.S. workers, with 9 in 10 reporting that the workplace affects their productivity. Respondents reported a 21% potential increase in productivity if spaces were better designed, translating into $377 billion in lost opportunity each year.

Findings from Gensler's 2005 U.K. Workplace Survey showed that workplace design is a significant factor to employees, and revealed that nearly 60% of the U.K. workforce felt that their space did not reflect or support their job function or creativity. In addition, the survey discovered the potential for a 19% increase in productivity through higher-performance spaces. This percentage increase translated into £137 billion pounds in overall lost profit each year.[22]

---

[21]Vischer, J (1999). Will this open space work? (1 May 2009) *Harvard Business Review*.
[22]Gensler (2008). Workplace Survey UK.

Privacy

While some employees prefer the privacy of an office, others like the feeling of an open space. Finding the right balance for all employees, within the financial and spatial constraints, is a challenge. But providing employees with a choice that allows them to adapt to their role needs makes sense. Companies today, such as Microsoft, have changed to a more adaptable design model: a mixture of 'hot-desks' and open-use offices that can be used according to the requirement of the employees; employees can use a private office or an interactive open space according to their needs and moods.[23]

Lighting

Lighting influences an individual's perception of work-related tasks, as well as affecting one's emotional and motivational state. In 2003, a field simulation study was conducted by the Lighting Research Center at Rensselaer Polytechnic Institute and National Research Council of Canada that indicated a causal relationship between lighting quality and worker satisfaction and motivation. Test subjects demonstrated improved satisfaction and motivation when provided with a new lighting design scheme.[24]

Noise

As more offices embrace open workspace designs noise control is emerging as a huge challenge. According to the American Society of Interior Designers (ASID), noise is the primary threat to office productivity in open environments: use of speaker phones, 'long-distance' discussions being conducted across the workplace or playing music out loud.[25] Workers in a noisy office can experience negative mood and make concentration worse. According to Cohen (1978) and Karasek and Theorell (1990), noise may also degrade performance via disruption and probably add to job-related stress. Hence, contributing to environmental and job dissatisfaction, office noise

---

[23]Microsoft moves into a new world of work. The Fifth Conference; http://www.thefifthconference.com/topic/move/microsoft-moves-new-world-work.

[24]Wiedenkeller, K (2010). SVP, Human Resources, AMC Entertainment in 'Some like it hot? Work environments impact productivity' (4 May 2010). *Film Journal International*.

[25]Wiedenkeller, K (2010). SVP, Human Resources, AMC Entertainment in 'Some like it hot? Work environments impact productivity' (4 May 2010). *Film Journal International*.

may disrupt and deteriorate employees' job performance through stress, distraction or overload.[26]

Best Practices Case Study: Google

A playground for fostering innovation and well-being

'The campus looks more like an idyllic resort than an office complex where anyone ever gets work done. The centrepiece of the main quadrangle is a beach volleyball court that sees a lot of action throughout the day'.[27]

The Google offices in Mountain Dew, and all over the world, are designed to foster creativity and to move away from the harsh, personality-less décor of the classical office structure. The 'campus' at Mountain Dew in California contains 12 buildings, which people travel between by walking or by using bicycles that are provided by the company. Throughout the campus there are more than a dozen cafés where employees go to meet or take time out. The main restaurants have open bench seating to encourage people to intermingle. There are rooms allocated explicitly for brainstorming filled with gadgets or toys to encourage people to play and explore non-linear ideas.

Workplace design and the impact on well-being and performance

The design of the workplace plays an influential role in shaping our desire to work in a particular organisation and in moulding our motivation at work. A report by the European Agency for Safety and Health at Work concluded that a healthy work environment can have 'a positive impact not only on safety and health performance but also on company productivity' and that a poor environment 'can lead to a competitive disadvantage impairing the firm's status among stakeholders'.[28]

---

[26] Chew Kok Wai, Poon Wai Ching, and Mohd. Fairuz Abd. Rahim. Working environment and stress: A survey on Malaysian employees in commercial banks. *Malaysian Management Review*; http://mgv.mim.edu.my/MMR/0606/060603.Htm.

[27] Deutschman, A (2005). Can Google stay Google (1 August 2005). *Fast Company*; http://www.fastcompany.com/magazine/97/open_google.html.

[28] Wiedenkeller, K (2010). SVP, Human Resources, AMC Entertainment in 'Some like it hot? Work environments impact productivity' (4 May 2010). *Film Journal International.*

Best Practices Case Study: Mayo Clinic

A design that is worlds apart from the clinical look of a hospital

In the Mayo Clinic, there is an environment of comfort and tradition that is worlds apart from the institutional atmosphere of many modern hospitals: fine art hangs on walls; doctors see patients in private offices — cosy spaces decorated with personal items — rather than in sterile white-and-chrome exam rooms;[29] and there are design features such as an indoor waterfall, a glass sculpture, and a wall of windows facing onto a garden or a mountain range.[30] There are multiple employee cafeterias offering healthy meal choices and cooking demonstrations.[31]

A study of nearly 4,000 employees in the year 2000 at the Polaroid Corporation documented a reduction in absenteeism through the use of enhanced ventilation using outdoor air. In 2003, a field simulation study was conducted by the Lighting Research Center at Rensselaer Polytechnic Institute and National Research Council of Canada that indicated a causal relationship between lighting quality and worker satisfaction and motivation.[32] A good environment has also been found to support a sense of well-being.

Zoom on ... Well-being at Work: the Impact of the Environs on Mood

The environs have also been found to affect mood. According to Nancy Etcoff, Center for Aesthetics and Well-Being at MGH, settings that combine 'prospect and refuge' seem to support a sense of well-being.[33]

---

[29]Roberts, P (1999). The agenda — Total teamwork (31 March 1999). *Fastcompany*.

[30]Berry, L and N Bendapudi (2003). Clueing in customers. *Harvard Business Review*, February.

[31]Mayo Clinic, Time off and work-life balance benefits; http://www.mayoclinic.org/jobs-rst/timeoff.html.

[32]Wiedenkeller, K (2010). SVP, Human Resources, AMC Entertainment in 'Some like it hot? Work environments impact productivity' (4 May 2010). *Film Journal International*; http://www.filmjournal.com/filmjournal/content_display/columns-and-blogs/the-people-factor/e3i7b2c50df9c8f86ff8be25b86bc20bd72.

[33]Lambert, C (2007). The science of happiness (January–February 2007). *Harvard Magazine*, p. 26.

According to Nancy Etcoff, 'Building windowless, nature-less, isolated offices full of cubicles ignores what people actually want. A study of patients hospitalised for gall-bladder surgery compared those whose rooms looked out on a park with those facing a brick wall. The park-view patients used less pain medication, had shorter stays, and complained less to their nurses. Ignoring the basic needs... We ignore our nature at our own peril.'

The Non-physical Working Environment

The non-physical working environment — the general rules and regulations, the way things are done in the office, the managerial pressure — contributes to an employee's psychological attitude towards work. These codes of behaviour can influence morale, motivation and can contribute to the existence, or not, of stress in the working environment.

A working environment with a casual dress code is increasingly becoming a factor that contributes to workplace attitudes. Google argues that 'You can be serious without a suit'.[34] Southwest Airlines introduced the casual dress code in year 1992 as a reward to employees for winning the Triple Crown. When the Triple Crown was again won the following year, and the year after, it was decided that the casual attire had become institutionalised and reflected the type of fun attitude that makes the business so successful 'Work at a place where wearing pants is optional'.[35]

Zoom on... Stress

Stress occurs where demands made on individuals do not match the resources available or meet the individual's needs and motivation... stress will be the result if the workload is too large for the number of workers and time available. Equally, a boring or repetitive task which does not use the potential skills and experience of some individuals will cause them stress'.[36]

---

[34]The ten things we know to be true. Google Website; http://www.google.com/corporate/tenthings.html.

[35]Freiberg, K and J Freiberg (1996). *Nuts! Southwest Airlines' Crazy Recipe for Business and Personal Success*. Austin: Bard Press, Inc.

[36]Raymond (2000). Stress the real millennium bug, Trades Union Congress.

Stress has been predicted to become the most *dangerous risk to business* in the early part of the 21st century. Stress is the result of an imbalance between our inner resources and skills on one hand, and pressures we encounter and support received to deal with these pressures.[37]

The CIPD annual absence management surveys show that stress is one of the most important reasons behind sickness from work and stress-related absence is increasing; other research conducted by CIPD in 2007 found that the average length of time someone takes off work with stress is 21 days. *In the UK one in five workers report feeling extremely stressed at work*; and self-reported work-related stress, depression or anxiety account for an estimated 10.5 million reported lost working days per year in Britain.[38]

Yet, it is important to note that pressure, often confused with stress, is not negative unless it becomes excessive. Up to a certain point, an increase in pressure can stimulate motivation and improve performance.[39]

According to Healthy Companies International, a U.S.-based management consultancy, nearly half of the 492 working Americans they recently surveyed said the current level of tension in their workplace was 'just right'. The study suggests that a productive workplace has to have a certain level of tension or energy.[40]

Best Practices Case Study: Bristol

Bristol University creates a Positive working environment strategy[41]

University College of Bristol is one of the Top 10 universities in the UK. It aims to 'nurture the collegial atmosphere that makes it a true community as well as an ambitious and challenging place to be'.

---

[37] James, K and T Arroba (1999). *Energizing the Workplace: A Strategic Response to Stress.* Aldershot, Brookfield, VT: Gower.

[38] Health and Safety Executive (2007). Stress-related and Psychological Disorders. Available at: http://www.hse.gov.uk/statistics/causdis/stress.htm.

[39] Taylor, R (2002). *The Future of Work-Life Balance.* Swindon, UK: Economic and Social Research Council.

[40] A 'Tension' Deficit? (April 2010) *HR Online*; http://www.hreonline.com/HRE/story.jsp?storyId=400272980.

[41] Bristol University: http://www.bris.ac.uk.

The impetus for change began with the conviction that a well-motivated workforce will lead to a successful organisation: attracting and retaining excellent people is considered key to long-term success. In 2000–2003, the University asked its staff what they thought of the university as an employer. There was an 'unease' among staff as to how they were valued as employees and people by the university. The Positive Working Environment initiative was adopted by the university with the aim of 'making working life productive, rewarding, enjoyable and healthy' for all colleagues.

Action related to the Positive Working Environment strategy is outlined through a series of five 'commitments' to staff. 'In essence, all of this investment is about creating an environment in which great research and inspiring teaching, within and across disciplines, are most likely to happen. However, success is not only about creating state-of-the-art laboratories and smart seminar rooms with all the latest equipment. It is, first and foremost, about attracting, supporting and retaining truly outstanding staff and students — ones who seek and can use what one might call 'the freedom to fly'.

Bristol University is the third best research institution to work at outside the United States for life scientists, according to a 'Best Places to Work in Academia' survey conducted by *The Scientist* magazine. Bristol University was awarded the 2009 Global Human Resource Development Awards from the International Federation of Training and Development Organisations Ltd (IFTDO) and the Outstanding Human Resource Initiative Award at the Times Higher Education Leadership and Management Awards 2009 ceremony.

5.4.2. *Working Conditions*

'The pay is good and I can walk to work.'

John F. Kennedy

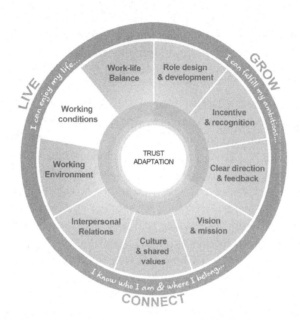

Good working conditions are an important criterion for employee satisfaction and help to create the conditions propitious for motivation at work. Once basic conditions are met, such as a salary and an employment status that provides comfortable and secure living conditions, people look to other needs and desires which stimulate motivation.

Definition of Working Conditions:

> The working conditions refer to the compensation and benefits provided by the company; the employment status of the employee and the security of the job; company policies and the legal framework that protects the worker; and the support systems in the company.

At the beginning of the 20th century, the International Labor Organisation established a charter on social justice and labour conditions. Central to this charter was the principle that 'the labor of a human being should not be treated as merchandise or an article of commerce'.[42] Yet, today the standard for adequate working conditions varies greatly from one role to another, from one industry to another, and from country to country. Individual working conditions are very closely linked to the principle of fairness; the individual may decide to seek work elsewhere if compensation or conditions are not perceived as fair.

> '*If people aren't compensated adequately and fairly, you don't get motivation. You will only get minimal effort to keep from getting fired. But if you pay people fairly, it takes the issue of compensation off the table, and they think about the work instead of the money.*'
>
> *Daniel Pink*

Compensation, benefits, employment status and security

Job security and the total compensation and benefits package of a job are important factors that contribute to the satisfaction of the employee.

Compensation

Pay is inevitably the central issue in the provision of good working conditions. It is the chief reason why most of us go to work in the first place and can be a significant cause of demotivation if our pay is perceived as unfair; yet, once a satisfactory and fair level of compensation is received, it can be argued that it no longer acts as the main driver of motivation at work. On the economic side, as wages represent an important part of labour costs and are an essential variable for companies' competitiveness, remuneration levels need to be carefully managed by companies by reconciling employee needs with the financial feasibility and return on investment.

Zoom on . . . The Importance of Pay

An interesting survey has been conducted three times since 1949 and each time the results have been the same. They demonstrated the discrepancy between what managers believe employees want, and what the employees

---

[42] World of Work, The Magazine of the ILO Issue 57, September 2006; http://www.ilo.org/wcmsp5/groups/public/—dgreports/—dcomm/documents/publication/dwcms_080598.pdf.

themselves say they want. Pay and job security were the two items that managers believed employees most valued. Employees, conversely, always cited 'feeling appreciated' and 'feeling informed' as the most important factors for job satisfaction.[43]

The U.S. Department Labor Statistics also show the number one reason employees leave organisations is that they 'don't feel appreciated'.[44]

Best Practices Case Study: Mayo Clinic

Compensation at Mayo Clinic: 'A disincentive system that works'

A competitive, market-leading salary is offered at Mayo; however, the maximum salary is reached in five years with annual increases over the five-year period. For instance, a 38-year-old endocrinologist in her fifth year at Mayo would earn the same salary as a 62-year-old endocrinologist who had been practicing for 32 years, although the long-term employee would earn more vacation time.[45]

According to one surgeon at the Mayo Clinic, 'Our system removes a set of perverse incentives and permits us to make all clinical decisions on the basis of what is best for the patient. Angioplasty versus surgery? The question has nothing to do with who gets paid what'.[46]

In Mayo Clinic, 'People who do exceptional work may be glad to be paid and even gladder to be well paid, but they do not work to collect a pay check. They work because they love what they do'.[47]

The role of compensation in motivation was often debated by Frederick Herzberg and was measured in his two-factor theory. He said that in cases where salary was identified as a cause of dissatisfaction, it essentially revolved around the unfairness of the wage system within the company. Conversely, salary was mentioned as one of the factors causing satisfaction

---

[43]Kouzes, J and B Posner (1999). *Encouraging the Heart*. San Francisco, CA: Jossey-Bass.

[44]Gostick, A and C Elton (2009). *The Carrot Principle*. London: Simon & Schuster.

[45]Financial and Retirement Benefits. Mayo Clinic Website; http://www.mayoclinic.org/jobs-rst/financial.html.

[46]Berry, L (2004). Leadership lessons from Mayo Clinic. *Organizational Dynamics*, 33(3), 228–242.

[47]Berry, L and K Seltman (2008). *Management Lessons from Mayo Clinic*. New York: McGraw Hill, pp. 120–121.

when it was associated with a person's achievement on the job. It was a form of recognition; it meant more than money — it meant a job well done. It meant that the individual was progressing in his work.[48] Other authors highlight the limited motivational power of money: 'The difference between an annual income of $5,000 and one of $50,000 is dramatic, but going from $50,000 to $50 million will not dramatically affect happiness. It's like eating pancakes: the first one is delicious, the second one is good, the third OK. By the fifth pancake, you're at a point where an infinite number more pancakes will not satisfy you to any greater degree. But no one stops earning money or striving for more money after they reach $50,000'.[49]

Spotlight on the Theory: Equity and Organisational Justice

John Stacey Adams (1965); Jerald Greenberg (1987)

Maintaining an equitable and transparent system is key to establishing perceptions of fairness in the organisation that helps maintain employee commitment and contributes to job satisfaction.

Employees evaluate their treatment in terms of inputs (what they put into the job: hard work, skill level, tolerance, enthusiasm, etc.) and outputs (what they receive in return for the job: salary, benefits, intangibles such as recognition, etc.) and compare this evaluation to their 'reference group': peers, co-workers, family... Perceptions of inequitable treatment may lead to dissatisfaction and demotivation.[50]

Greenberg complemented equity theory by building on organisational justice concepts. He suggested that when assessing the fairness of organisational decisions (e.g., the allocation of pay and other resources), employees take into account not only what those decisions are (i.e., outcomes, such as pay and performance ratings), but also the manner in which those decisions are made (i.e., procedures).

Benefits

Employee benefits represent virtually any form of compensation provided in a form other than direct wages. Benefits are often an important

---

[48]Herzberg, F (1979). The wise old Turk. *Harvard Business Review*, 52, 70–81.

[49]Lambert, C (2007). The science of happiness (January–February 2007). *Harvard Magazine*; http://harvardmagazine.com/2007/01/the-science-of-happiness.html.

[50]Adams, JS (1965). Inequity in social exchange. *Advances in Experimental Social Psychology*, 62, 335–343.

consideration for people for joining the organisation and therefore play an important role in attracting personnel. Benefits are a tool used to attract, retain and motivate employees, and also to enable the company to meet its social obligations.[51]

Actual benefit plans that are classified as employee benefits today can be traced back to the end of the 18th century. The first recorded profit-sharing plan was set up by Albert Gallatin in his glassworks factory and the first private pension plan was started by the American Express Company in 1875. Today benefit plans play an important role in facilitating the needs of employees and they are supported by government legislation. Benefits used by companies today include legally required benefits such as Social Security and unemployment compensation; pensions, life insurance and disability payments; payments for time not worked such as sick and vacation time; and profit-sharing plans, awards and bonuses.[52]

Flexible or cafeteria-style benefit plans enable employees to receive more value from their benefits, because they can be tailored to an individual's needs. A flexible benefit plan allows employees to become more aware and appreciative of their benefits, thus increasing morale and productivity. Flexible compensation plans can also be used to convert earnings into tax-free benefits, thereby producing a more valuable total reward package. However, good communication of the flexible benefit plan is critical in order for employees to benefit from it. It is also important to discuss the plan with employees to understand what they like or dislike about the program and to adapt it accordingly to ensure that it is valued by the employee.[53]

Employment status and security

Employment security can play a role in creating a trusting relationship between the employer and the employee. Siemens have introduced 'jobs for life' for their 128,000 German workers,[54] presumably to inspire a greater loyalty and commitment from their workers.

---

[51]Marsh, B and H Kleiner (1998). An overview of trends in employee benefits programmes. *Management Research News*, 21(4/5), 23–29.
[52]Marsh, B and H Kleiner (1998). An overview of trends in employee benefits programmes. *Management Research News*, 21(4/5), 23–29.
[53]Forbes (2006). The best benefits package for small biz, in Forbes.com; http://www. forbes.com/2006/10/06/aetna-unitedhealth-retirement-ent-hr-cx_mf_1006benefits.html.
[54]Tobak, S (2010). Jobs for Life: If It Works in Germany, Why Not America?

Zoom on ... The Rising Wave of Worker Militancy in Asia

'The ability of employers to pay very low wages is diminishing.'

In China, rising tensions between employers and employees have led to increases in labour disputes. Labour disputes in Guangdong in the first quarter of 2009 had risen by nearly 42% over the same period in 2008. In Zhejiang, the year-on-year increase was almost 160%. Workers have been emboldened by a law introduced in January 2008 aimed at strengthening their contractual rights. Foxconn, the world's largest contract electronics manufacturer, raised wages 30 percent following a spate of suicides in one of its large southern China factory complexes (Figure 5.1).

In Bangladesh, the world's lowest paid garment workers, who make clothes for Western brands, recently revolted against pay standards, despite receiving an 80 percent pay rise (from $23 per month to $43). The wage rise was considered wholly inadequate in view of the rising cost of living; the Prime Minister of Bangladesh called the current minimum wage 'not only insufficient, but inhuman.'

In Cambodia, the minimum wage was recently raised by 21% — from $50 per month to $61. Vietnam recorded 200 strikes last year by workers hit by inflation of 9 per cent. For example, almost 10,000 workers walked out of a Taiwan-owned shoe factory in April, seeking better pay.

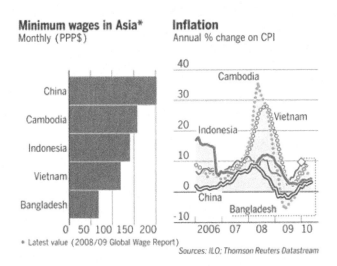

Figure 5.1   Global wage report.

In 2008, Jakarta raised the local minimum wage by 10 percent to nearly $100 a month; although wages in the country's remoter regions are often half this figure. Indonesia has also recorded an increase in strikes at textile factories, including a one-day stoppage last month in Bandung, where 40,000 workers from various companies walked out in protest against rising electricity prices. In India, too, Nokia, Bosch, Hyundai, and Volvo and countless local companies have all faced rising industrial unrest.

Workers' wages are indeed in the process of development in Asia; yet, as one labour rights activist claims, 'There are no industrial relations, the whole attitude is arrogant and feudal. Owners and government think they are helping the workers. The workers are not treated like workers — they are treated like beggars.'

In the past, with an abundant supply of workers available, employees who complained know that they would be thrown out of the job. Nowadays, manufacturers too are realising that there are other benefits by increasing worker wages, namely, higher worker retention and increased efficiency.[55]

Support systems

Business and human rights

All companies have a direct responsibility to respect human rights in their operations, and some feel they also have a moral responsibility in promoting respect for the rights of employees. Organisations that effectively act to prevent involvement in human rights violations/abuses and address problems that can arise provide employees and stakeholders with a positive and safe framework of working conditions.

Zoom on ... Corporate Social Responsibility

Human Rights First (2006)

The International Labor Organisation has articulated labour rights standards for over 80 years; yet these assume that national governments

---

[55]Kazmin, A (2010). Asian labour militancy on the rise (18 August 2010). *Financial Times*; http://www.ft.com/cms/s/0/cdca5598-aae8-11df-9e6b-00144feabdc0.html.

will enforce them. Unfortunately, many governments lack the capacity and often the will to do so.

Such consequences have sparked a growing public demand for corporations to take responsibility for a range of human rights and environmental problems in countries in which they operate. The challenge is to create accountability — independent, transparent and enforceable mechanisms for ensuring that human rights standards protect ordinary people.

Support systems

Many organisations today offer services that support employees' intangible needs. Employees may face pressure in both their work and personal life and introducing a comprehensive system of support may help to protect the well-being of staff members. Ongoing support for employees can also help to counteract organisational problems such as absenteeism and poor performance.

Best Practices Case Study: Employee Assistance Programs

Employee assistance programs are intended to help employees deal with personal problems that might adversely impact their work performance, health and well-being.

HCL offer a counselling service called 'MITR' Counselling Service: It lends a helping hand to all HCL employees and their family members by providing them expert counselling 24/7 on any issue concerning them.[56]

Sodexo's LifeWorks program provides personal and professional resources for U.S. employees and their families, for better living. Services are available 24 hours a day, 7 days a week. Counsellors can help people research various topics, and a website also offers resources, chats, podcasts and workshops on a large number of topics.

---

[56] Dey, P (2009). HCL technologies: The transformation journey, January 2009.

5.4.3. *Work–life Balance*

'It's all about quality of life and finding a happy balance between work and friends and family.'

Philip Green

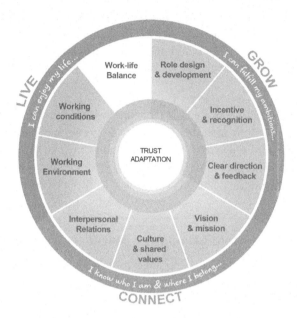

Today, there is a greater need for managers to be aware of an employee's whole life needs. Work–life balance is achieved when an individual's right to a fulfilled life inside and outside work is accepted and supported, to the mutual benefit of the individual, business and society. Helping to support and understand employee work–life balance needs can help employers to develop a more committed and productive workforce.

Definition of Work–Life Balance:

Work–life balance measures refer to working practices that assist workers in achieving a balance between employment (working life, career, ambition) and private life (family, leisure, pleasure, etc.), leading to being able to enjoy an optimal quality of life overall. Individual needs, experiences and goals, define the relative importance of work and personal life for a particular individual.

The chief areas where the organisation can implement work–life balance measures are in terms of time management, and resource and referral services. It should first be noted that the different legislation environments in which a company is based will mean that some countries are more favourable to employee work–life balance than others; yet many companies go above and beyond the legal requirement.[57]

Zoom on... The Impact of Legislation on Work–Life Balance Measures

The great diversity of actions implemented by businesses is largely a result of the institutional context, the various forms of social regulation and the collective representations of the family in its environment. Companies are thus subject to highly varied pressures across countries or sectors in relation to these policies.[58]

Time management

In 1930, John Maynard Keynes visualised a world in which work would largely be replaced by leisure. He hypothesised a three-hour shift and a fifteen-hour working week by the year 2030.[59] Our society today is far removed from the vision of John Maynard Keynes; yet the merits of a reduced working week have not ceased to be a topic of discussion. The business world today has to contend with greater challenges to increase productivity and create value through innovation and improved economies of scale; otherwise, companies simply cannot compete in the global marketplace. Because global wage standards are on an upward trend, the gains necessarily have to come from increased productivity or innovation. And thus, there is a certain pressure on employees to be creative, more productive and to deliver results. This pressure can have an impact on the time that people spend at work.

Zoom... Working Hours

According to the International Labor Organisation, some 22% of the world's workers were working more than 48 hours per week at the turn

---

[57]Think Tank Européen Pour la Solidarité (2010). *Work Life Balance*.
[58]For more detailed information on businesses in Member States: 'Employers little involved in reconciling work/family life, according to a study by the INED', which shows that there is progress still to be made in France on the part of employers.
[59]World of Work Magazine No. 57, September 2006. An honest day's work? Considering the nebulous notion of today's work-life balance; http://www.ilo.org/wow/Featuredbook/lang–en/WCMS_081382/index.htm.

of the 21st century.[60] In most European countries, the work week is 35 hours, while Canadians clock about 40 hours. The average workweek in South Korea and Japan is 30% longer.[61]

And despite the European Union (EU) initiating 'Working Time Regulations', which set a threshold for a 48-hour work week, working for more than 48 hours is relatively common in today's society.[62] Yet, atypical and unpredictable work schedules are on the rise worldwide, due to an increasingly connected, responsive and demanding global economy.[63] The increasing demands on employees is expressed by Robert Taylor in *The Future of Work-Life Balance*: 'As the twenty-four hour, seven-day working week gains ascendancy, the possibility of achieving a satisfactory work-life balance is proving an elusive goal for more and more people'.[64]

Zoom... The Pajama Workforce

Has technology and telecommuting produced a new type of worker?

To some people working from home may sound like a dream come true. No 'mad dash' in the morning to run out of the door; more free hours in the day and a later alarm clock setting; no encounters with angry, impatient commuters to set a negative tone to your day; and all of the other potential joys that working from home represents. But is this newfound freedom all it's cracked up to be? Some of the pitfalls identified include: working in pajamas, a lack of routine and boundaryless working day, weight gain due to decrease in movement and continual access to

---

[60]Gavin, J and R Mason (2004). The virtuous organization: The value of happiness in the workplace. *Organizational Dynamics*, 33(4), 379–392.

[61]Williams, R (2010). The productivity paradox: When is less more? *The Financial Post*; http://business.financialpost.com/2010/06/24/the-productivity-paradox-when-is-less-more/.

[62]Maxwell, GA (2005). Checks and balances: The role of managers in work–life balance policies and practices. *Journal of Retailing and Consumer Services*, 12, 179–189.

[63]An honest day's work? Considering the nebulous notion of today's work-life balance (September 2006). World of Work Magazine No. 57; http://www.ilo.org/wow/Featuredbook/lang–en/WCMS_081382/index.htm.

[64]Taylor, R (2002). *The Future of Work-Life Balance*. Swindon, UK: Economic and Social Research Council.

food; working in a non-productive space; and never 'switching off' from work.[65]

Without a culture of strong accountability, collaboration, trust and personal responsibility, remote work doesn't work. People need clear goals, deadlines and performance metrics. Jack Welch, the former CEO of GE known for his radical views on management, believes that work-life balance privileges should be earned by first showing commitment to work, 'If you don't deliver, you don't earn the flexibility.'

Work–life balance does not mean a perfect balance between the time you spend at work and time outside of work; it is about making sure that people have the flexibility or support when they need it, to enable them to put forth their best effort at work. If someone is commuting two hours to work each morning, perhaps it would make good sense to consider either flexibility or telecommuting.[66]

Zoom ... Company Strategies for Time Management

Flexible working hours: Flexible schedules, management by results rather than presence, annualised hours or time-savings accounts.

Flexible leave arrangements: Apart from statutory entitlements (such as annual leave and maternity), other leave arrangements include paternity leave, emergency leave, employment or career break, sabbaticals, exam and study leave.

Reduced working time: Part-time work, on a fixed basis or for a limited period with right to return to full-time work; job-sharing.

Flexible location: e-working, virtual teams.

Best Practices Case Study: Flexible Working in Microsoft

Flexibility as a tool to adapt to new business and employee needs

Gone are the days of sitting behind the same desk for 50 years, plugging away at the same tasks day in and day out. *With traffic congestion and*

---

[65]5 bad work at home habits: Are you guilty? http://freelancefolder.com/5-bad-work-at-home-habits-are-you-guilty/.

[66]Work-life balance defined: What it really means (2003); http://www.worklifebalance.com/worklifebalancedefined.html.

public transport issues spiralling out of control, how can employees be expected to sit in front of a desk for 8 hours after wrestling their way through traffic jams? Microsoft's answer to this is simple: 'employees don't get used to their work environment, it gets used to them.' Employees can decide for themselves where and how they want to work.

No employee has a fixed desk or phone and *all staff use laptops to work at a time and a place they find suitable.* The objective was to redesign the office environment for what it is in reality used for — today it is mainly meetings.[67]

A key issue with the new way of working — from anywhere on any device — was the attitudinal change required in the company. However, this process was much more straightforward than anticipated: 'Animals that have their cages opened and are allowed to run free almost never immediately dash off into the savannah'. Monitoring an employee's performance isn't necessarily dependent on hours spent at the office. Employees were taught how to work productively from remote locations and the change in Microsoft has begun to pay off: *employees are enthusiastic, productivity is on the up, and, perhaps not surprisingly, they won the Great Places to Work award again in 2009.*[68]

The value for the employer

There is a lot of debate on the pros and cons of work–life balance practices today and it is perceived by some as being 'anti-business'.[69] Are workers too demanding? Is the personal life of staff the concern of the organisation? And yet, stress is a growing concern in our society today and can have a negative impact on employee well-being, absenteeism and more.

Work–life balance policies that allow people to balance work with the other dimensions of their lives has a beneficial impact on both the business and individual well-being. The benefit for businesses include increased productivity, improved retention, lower rates of absenteeism, reduced overheads and a more motivated and satisfied workforce.[70]

---

[67] Microsoft moves into a new world of work. The Fifth Conference; http://www.thefifthconference.com/topic/move/microsoft-moves-new-world-work.
[68] Microsoft moves into a new world of work. The Fifth Conference; http://www.thefifthconference.com/topic/move/microsoft-moves-new-world-work.
[69] Muktarsingh, N (2003). Business Briefing (1 March 2003). *Financial Mail*, Sunday.
[70] The Work Foundation Factsheet (2008); http://www.theworkfoundation.com/difference/e4wlb/factsheet.aspx.

Zoom on ... The Value of Work–Life Balance for Employers

By facilitating the course of various moments of life, work–life balance policies promote employee well-being, by reducing stress and disruptions of work on private life and vice versa. As a result, employees are *more engaged in their professional activity.*[71]

By enabling a smoother transition between work life and private and family life, as well as providing a quality work environment, there are undeniable advantages for employees. It is easier to *attract and retain* a wide breadth of employees, particularly skilled workers. Companies providing work–life balance policies experience less employee turnover, which lowers recruitment and training costs.[72] *By allowing greater flexibility in the workplace*, there are *lower incidences of absenteeism* and lateness for work.[73]

While work–life balance measures may seem like a costly expense, there are many gains for the employer. Practices such as flexibility are important for attracting high-calibre candidates to the organisation: good work–life policies demonstrate that the organisation is a supportive and positive place to work. The 2003 UK Graduate Careers survey showed that graduates value flexibility more than pay when looking at prospective employers.[74]

Zoom on ... The Productivity Gains

A survey of 1,008 U.S. male workers between the ages of 20 and 39 found that spending more time with their family was more important than challenging work or earning a high salary. In the survey, 70% said they would be willing to give up some pay in exchange for more family time.[75]

---

[71]Think Tank Européen Pour la Solidarité (2010). *Work Life Balance.*
[72]Think Tank Européen Pour la Solidarité (2010). *Work Life Balance.*
[73]Think Tank Européen Pour la Solidarité (2010). *Work Life Balance.*
[74]University of Bristol; http://www.bris.ac.uk/pwe/worklife2.html.
[75]Work and Family Connection (2005). *The Most Important Work-Life-Related Studies.* Minnetonka, MN: Work and Family Connection.

The survey also found that 77% of the workers who experience their culture as being supportive say it is highly likely they will stay, compared with 41% who do not describe their culture as supportive. What do they consider supportive? More than twice as many respondents with access to flexible work arrangements are highly satisfied with their jobs, as are more than three times as many who have supervisor support.[76]

Another U.S. study found that 55% of workers who were offered a child-care subsidy were better able to concentrate at work and 48% were more likely to stay. While 19% reported fewer days absent from work, three-fourths felt that the subsidy has improved their job performance.[77]

A study conducted in Germany demonstrated that implementation of work–life balance policies can improve the company's overall performance: research commissioned by the Ministry of Families conducted by the Prognos Research Institute concludes that the introduction of work–family measures adopted by companies can save 50% of the costs incurred by the absence of attention to the family constraints of employees.[78]

Best Practices Case Study: University of Bristol

Improving employee satisfaction and motivation through work–life balance practices

Addressing employee dissatisfaction and stress

In the University of Bristol, a survey revealed that a large number of staff were unsatisfied with their work–life balance and felt that they worked excessive hours. As a result, the university is trying to address this issue in a number of different ways: information, training and projects to make work processes more efficient.

---

[76]Work and Family Connection (2005). *The Most Important Work-Life-Related Studies.* Minnetonka, MN: Work and Family Connection.
[77]Work and Family Connection (2005). *The Most Important Work-Life-Related Studies.* Minnetonka, MN: Work and Family Connection.
[78]Think Tank Européen Pour la Solidarité (2010). Work Life Balance.

'*Making working life productive, rewarding, enjoyable and healthy*'

The university has introduced a Staff Counselling Service and a 'Work Life Balance Center', which offers staff a brief guide to active living and workload management. They use a specific tool to create a personal work–life balance profile for staff.

Strategies

A range of support systems that include flexible time and financial help are available for those with caring responsibilities. This includes tax credits for child-care and nursery education grants, how to take time off work to care for a relative, in addition to the University Maternity and Paternity Leave schemes. University of Bristol is actively trying to help people to achieve a better work–life balance through initiatives such as: 'stress management', 'knock that fatigue on the head', 'improving your time management', and 'improving and maintaining your performance'.

Resource and Referral Services

Zoom on... Company Strategies for Work–Life Benefits

Benefits in-kind: Companies can provide their employees with benefits in-kind by providing or assisting with child-care facilities for their children; creation of a day-care centre; provision of a corporate concierge service; assistance in obtaining housing at affordable cost; establishment of a cafeteria or subsidisation of a company restaurant and others.

Financial benefits: Companies also can promote work–life balance by granting financial benefits: aid that covers all employees (such as assistance with meals through restaurant vouchers, vacation vouchers, contributions to a mutual fund) and financial aids specifically designed to help families with child-care costs, educational assistance for children, bonuses (marriage, birth), the granting of additional compensation for maternity or paternity leave.

Best Practices Case Study: Mayo Clinic

Financial benefits

Mayo Clinic offers staff a Computers @ Home Service: a discount to purchase a new home computer, increase computer literacy and refurbish or recycle used computers; and Adoption Reimbursement.[79]

Benefits in-kind

Mayo Clinic offer staff legal services assistance related to purchasing a home, managing expenses, preparing a will, adopting a child and civil matters; and Mayo Classified Advertisements (free service for buying and selling personal items and services).[80]

Health and wellness

> ' We know that reasonably active people tend to be more positive about life and work than the inactive, so our aim is to encourage more staff to be more active more often, without it hurting!'
>
> *University of Bristol*

A poll was conducted by Schwartz (2010) on people's experience in the workplace. Of 1200 respondents, 60% said they took less than 20 minutes a day for lunch, 20% admitted they took less than 10 minutes and 25% said they never left their desks. That's consistent with a study by the American Dietetic Association, which found that 75% of office workers eat lunch at their desk at least two days a week.[81]

Gallup estimates that a 'suffering employee' — one with a low well-being score — costs their employer about US$28,800 a year in productivity lost because of sick leave. This is more than four times the US$6,168 for an employee of average well-being and 34 times that of an employee with the

---

[79] Mayo Clinic Website; http://www.mayoclinic.org/jobs-rst/family.html.
[80] Mayo Clinic Website; http://www.mayoclinic.org/jobs-rst/family.html.
[81] The productivity paradox: When is less more? (24 June 1020) *The Financial Post*; http://business.financialpost.com/2010/06/24/the-productivity-paradox-when-is-less-more/#ixzz10UFfNlBA.

highest level of well-being, who is likely to cost their employer just $840 a year in lost productivity.[82]

Taking vacation

Taking vacation time is an essential way for employees to recharge their batteries and give time to their life outside of work. Patterns in taking time off work for vacation vary greatly around the world as a result of different regulations and local practices. Furthermore, with many people now having perpetual access to emails via phones and laptops, it is increasingly difficult to 'switch off' from work.[83]

Travel website, Expedia.com, has compiled comparative international data on the scandal of 'vacation deprivation'. The data shows that in 2009 the average American adult received about 13 days of holiday, whereas the average Briton enjoyed a comfortable 26-day holiday. The average Frenchman spent 38 days in holiday. Conversely, more than one-third of Americans do not even take all the days they are allowed; according to Expedia, in 2009 Americans returned a total of 436 million unused vacation days.

Presenteeism

'Presenteeism' is the cost to the organisation of lost productivity, when physical and mental health issues interfere with the workers' ability to perform to his or her full potential.[84] It occurs when an employee attends work in spite of being sick. A Work Foundation survey reported that, in 2009, two out of five workers surveyed admitted to not having taken a day off sick in the previous 12 months. This follows another survey by healthcare provider SimplyHealth, which argued that fears over job security and redundancy during the recession had led to a sharp rise in presenteeism.[85]

---

[82] Businesses could do more to ensure staff thrive, improve well-being (17 June 2010). *The Business Times*;. http://business.asiaone.com/Business/News/Office/Story/A1Story20 100615-222171.html.

[83] The air-conditioned puritan (19 August 2009). *The Economist.*

[84] Humphrey BG (2010). Absenteeism and Disability Management — Effective Strategies Require Confronting the Elephants in the Room. HR Database; http://www.longwoods. com/content/21943.

[85] The end of the sick day (14 September 2009); https://www.simplyhealth.co.uk/sh/ pages/media-centre/press-release-article.jsp?articleId=239315.

Best Practices Case Study: University of Bristol

'Helping to empower individuals to achieve positive change'

Well Wednesdays

No lectures are time-tabled for most students on Wednesdays so that they can focus on inter-university sports competitions. The University of Bristol has decided to take Wednesdays one step further and encourage *everyone* at the University, staff and students, to make Wednesdays *Wellness Days* and do something positive for their health and well-being.[86]

Commute to work

Long-distance commuting is on the rise: one survey last year found 10% of Britons spending two or more hours a day on the road. Numerous studies[87] have shown commuting to have the most negative impact on happiness of all daily activities, linked with stress and social isolation, and often far outweighing the benefits.

The Swiss economists, Alois Stutzer and Bruno Frey, have called this the 'commuter's paradox': people underestimate the downsides of a long commute, while overestimating the upsides of their house location, for instance.[88] As the neuroscience writer Jonah Lehrer notes, that is partly because commuting, especially in car traffic, is unpredictable, so we never get used to it.[89]

Tailoring work–life balance to the different needs of employees

Work–life balance needs inevitably vary over time; from one day to the next and over the course of the employee lifetime. Having the right balance when an individual starts his career may change at a later stage if he starts a family. Supporting employees and understanding that at times they may

---

[86]University of Bristol Website; http://www.bris.ac.uk/sport/healthyliving/livewell/wellwednesdays/.

[87]Monitor, longer train commutes are more stressful, September 2006, 37(8) http://www.apa.org/monitor/sep06/commutes.aspx.

[88]Stress that doesn't pay: The commuting paradox; http://ideas.repec.org/p/zur/iewwpx/151.html.

[89]http://www.jonahlehrer.com/.

need flexibility will show them that the organisation cares about them; they in turn will be more willing to put in a good effort at work.[90]

5.5. Grow: I Can Fulfil My Ambitions...

The need to grow is one of the greatest drivers of motivation for people at work. As Abraham Maslow said, 'What a man can be, he must be. This need we call self-actualisation... If you deliberately plan on being less than you are capable of being, then I warn you that you'll be unhappy for the rest of your life'.[91] The need for fulfilment, or self-actualisation, is one for which we continue to strive throughout our lives. As Honoré de Balzac, the French 17th century author stated, 'An unfulfilled vocation drains the colour from a man's entire existence'.[92] 'Grow' recognises the human need for competence, progress and self-achievement and to find interest and meaning in work. Organisations that encourage a good person-role fit and provide opportunities for progression and challenge, responsibility,

---

[90]Work-life balance defined: What it really means (2003); http://www.worklifebalance. com/worklifebalancedefined.html.

[91]Maslow, A (1954). *Motivation and Personality*. New York: Harper and Row.

[92]Honoré de Balzac, Scenes de la vie Parisienne, *La Maison Nucingen*, 1838.

empowerment and growth have more committed and motivated employees. Goal-setting and feedback are other essential components for motivation, and they direct individual behavior towards the achievement of organisational goals. Incentives and recognition also play an important role in orienting, encouraging and sustaining motivation at work. We look at the driver of growth through the levers *Role Design & Development, Incentive & Recognition*, and *Clear Direction & Feedback*.

5.5.1.   *Role Design and Development*

> '*You do your best work if you do a job that makes you happy.*'
>
> Bob Ross

Interest in the work and opportunities for growth are acknowledged as two of the most powerful levers of motivation. Every organisation has the power to provide workers with opportunities to increase their interest in the role; to develop their competencies, to attach a sense of purpose and meaning to their work so that they may grow and progress in their role and in the organisation.

Definition of Role Design and Development:

Role design and development concern the job itself and the opportunities for progression in the role and in the organisation. A job can be designed to inspire a lasting interest and motivation for the function, to create variety and a sense of meaning for the task. Development of the individual over time creates a long-term interest and investment in the role by empowering the individual to take ownership and responsibility for the role. Providing training or support to help and encourage people to improve competencies is central. A coaching environment helps to unlock the true potential of the employee. It allows employees to use and develop their skills and help them to gain a sense of accomplishment in their work.

Interest in the work

'You don't enjoy what you're doing if you're just handing out peanuts and drinks. You enjoy it if you can be interactive, if you can have conversations, if they know your name. Other airlines don't have the sort of conversations with customers like we do.'

Colleen Barrett, Southwest Airlines

Findings suggest that interesting work is key to higher employee motivation; it is often ranked among the main motivators. Therefore job design — organising tasks, duties, responsibilities, methods and relationships of jobs into a productive unit of work — play a role in job satisfaction and employee motivation when they satisfy the personal needs of job holders as well as organisational requirements. Workers who are more interested in their jobs display more work commitment and experience lower turnover.[93]

Job-characteristic models identify important design characteristics of 'good' jobs. Meaningfulness of the work, autonomy and opportunities for growth are among those components that are likely to be positively received by employees and that affect motivation and performance.

Beyond job characteristics, what is important is person-job fit. Finding the right person for the right role is one of the prerequisites for ensuring that they will be motivated in the role. According to Teresa Amabile, one of the most efficacious things a manager can do to stimulate creativity and intrinsic motivation is 'the deceptively simple task of matching people with

---

[93] Jauch, LR and U Sekaran (1978). Employee orientation and job satisfaction among professional employees in hospitals. *Journal of Management*, 4(1), 43–56.

the right assignments'.[94] Managers can match people with jobs that play to their expertise and their skills in creative thinking, and ignite intrinsic motivation.

Person-job fit occurs when employees' knowledge, skills and abilities match with what the job requires, and when employee's needs, desires or preferences are met by the jobs that they perform. Hiring the right staff members is important; however, defining staff positions may be just as important to improve motivation and organisational functioning. It is important to note that individual responses to jobs vary. People bring a diverse range of skills and abilities to the workplace, together with a diverse range of experiences, aspirations and expectations. A job may be motivating to one person but not to someone else, and depending on how jobs are designed, they may provide more or less opportunity for employees to satisfy their job-related needs.[95]

Skill variety

> 'How do you work up the conviction and discipline you need to do tiresome, unglamorous tasks? Well, how did you get yourself through high school, college, your first boring entry-level job?'
>
> *Mark Jaffe*

Skill variety is the extent to which the work requires several activities for successful completion. The more skills involved the more meaningful the work. High levels of task rationalisation are associated with high levels of boredom, which in turn is associated with job dissatisfaction and counterproductive worker behavior (it should be noted that such jobs have appeal to some workers).

Skill variety can be enhanced in several ways. Job enlargement can be used to increase motivation by giving employee's more and varied tasks to broaden the scope of a job and extend the length of time he or she has to complete tasks. Job enrichment allows the employee to take on some responsibilities normally delegated to management, provided he is able and willing to, as it is important for employees to feel that they control their own actions. Job rotation allows an employee to work in different departments or jobs in an organisation to gain better insight into operations; this breaks the monotony of an otherwise routine job with little scope by shifting a

---

[94] Amabile, T (1998). *What Kills Creativity*. Cambridge, MA: Harvard Business Press.
[95] Kristof-Brown, A, R Zimmerman and E Johnson (2005). Consequences of individuals' fit at work: A meta-analysis of person–job, person–organization, person–group, and person–supervisor fit. *Personnel Psychology*, 58(2), 281–342.

person from job to job and allowing the opportunity to increase skills and knowledge.[96]

Many car-manufacturing plants, such as Toyota, Ferrari, and Volvo, have implemented some form of job-enrichment. The process is found to result in higher quality production, lower turnover and lower rates of absenteeism; yet, it may pose a challenge in terms of implementation costs and maintaining competitiveness.[97]

Best Practices Case Study: Mayo Clinic

Assignment rotation

Employees who fit well in the Mayo culture are resources that can often be reinvested in other more promising positions in the organisation.[98]

Administrators rotate every four to seven years, to broaden their experience base while providing the physician and the administrative unit new ideas and energy.

Physicians have multiple opportunities to serve on committees or task forces, especially those outside their comfort zones.[99]

Meaningfulness of the role

Employees who derive a sense of purpose and meaning from their job are more likely to be motivated to do well. Task identity and task significance positively impact this feeling. Task identity is about being responsible for a unit of work carried from start to finish and resulting in a tangible outcome, as a result of separation of duties and well-written job description for instance. The amount of impact a job has on other people, because it contributes to the success of the company or because it makes clients happy, indicates its task significance. Meaningfulness stimulates responsibility and leads to engagement.

Wrzesniewski (2003) connects employee well-being to the idea of work having meaning. She describes a hierarchy of the meaning of work ranging from a *'job'* at the low end, to the middle range idea of a *'career'* and the

[96] Richard Hackman, JR and GR Oldham (1976). Motivation through the design of work: Test of a theory. *Organizational Behavior and Performance*, 16, 250–279.

[97] Jang, JS, SC Rim and SC Park (2006). Reforming a conventional vehicle assembly plant for job enrichment. *International Journal of Production Research*, 44(4), 15, 703–713.

[98] Berry, L and K Seltman (2008). *Management Lessons from Mayo Clinic*. McGraw Hill: New York, p. 154.

[99] Executive Leadership (2009). Leadership checkup at the Mayo Clinic, August 2009.

highest level of meaning as a '*calling*'. She describes the positive relationship between an employee's sense of work as a calling and performance on the job. The hierarchy of job — career — calling is demonstrated in the fable about a man walking past a bricklayer and asking the bricklayer what he is doing. The worker responds by saying, 'I am laying bricks'. Dissatisfied with that response, the man proceeds to the next worker and asks him what he is doing. He responds that he is building a wall. Still dissatisfied, the man moves on to a third worker and asks the same question. The worker stands up straight, looks the man in the eye and proudly states, 'I'm building a cathedral'.[100]

Spotlight on the Theory: Job Characteristics Theory

J. Richard Hackman and Greg R. Oldham (1980)

When jobs are structured in a way that intrinsic rewards result from performance, then the job itself can be a very effective motivator.

Hackman and Oldham state that there are three main characteristics for the job content to be a source of motivation:

— The individual must receive meaningful feedback about his performance.
— The job must be perceived by the individual as requiring the use of his abilities or skills in order for him to perform the job effectively; valuing an employee's skills can lead to feelings of accomplishment and growth.
— The individual must feel that he has a high degree of self-control over setting his own goals and deciding how he will achieve these goals.[101]

For this to occur, jobs must be enlarged horizontally and vertically:

— Increased variety of tasks — for instance, for an employee working on a production line, a system of job rotation can prevent task boredom and stimulate interest in the job;

---

[100]Won-joo, Yun and F Mulhern (2009). Leadership and the Performance of People in Organizations: Enriching Employees and Connecting People. *Forum for People Performance Management and Measurement Publication*, November.
[101]Vroom, VH and EL Deci (1970). *Management and Motivation*. Baltimore: Penguin Education.

— Increased responsibility or autonomy — for instance, many companies have increased the interaction with employees to incorporate their opinions in terms of decision-making.[102]

Opportunities for Competence, Growth, Development and Autonomy

Providing opportunities for development is one of the most meaningful ways of demonstrating to an individual that the organisation is willing to invest in him or her; this investment helps to convey the value, raising esteem and in turn fostering the engagement and commitment towards organisational goals. If people are given opportunities to progress, they will feel more loyal and committed and will also be motivated to improve their current competencies and behaviour. When workers are more involved in job-related decisions they respond by showing greater involvement and motivation.[103]

Accomplishment and Progress

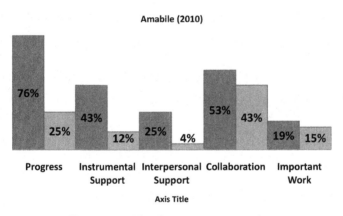

Figure 5.2   What happens on a great day.

Feeling like one has accomplished something can be a very motivating factor for future behaviour.

[102]Vroom, VH and EL Deci (1970). *Management and Motivation.* Baltimore: Penguin Education.
[103]Wiley, C (1997) What motivates employees according to over 40 years of motivation surveys. *International Journal of Manpower,* 18(3), 263–280.

A study by Teresa Amabile, which looked at people's emotions and their feelings about their work, the feeling of progress corresponded with 76% of people's 'best days', when their reported moods were most buoyant, and on only 25% of their worst. On days when workers have the sense they are making headway in their jobs, or when they receive support that helps them overcome obstacles, their emotions are most positive and their drive to succeed is at its peak. On days when they feel they are 'spinning their wheels' or encountering obstructions to meaningful accomplishment, their moods and motivation are lowest (Figure 5.2).[104]

Empowerment

Organisational designs that permit greater participation in decision making and greater flexibility in doing one's job have been found to be positively associated with employee satisfaction, quality of work life and organisational effectiveness.[105]

Spotlight on the Theory: Self-Determination

Edward L. Deci & Richard M. Ryan (1981 to 1991)

Intrinsic motivation is based chiefly in the innate human needs to feel autonomous and competent. Self-determination also impacts the quality of extrinsic motivation.

According to Deci and Ryan, each individual develops two needs in tandem: the need to feel competent, and the need for self-determination. Both are key to experience intrinsic motivation and react positively to extrinsic motivation:

Self-determination and feeling of competency are two of the main factors that lead to intrinsic motivation, and thus create employee enjoyment and interest in the task. Self-determination occurs when the employee experiences choice in his actions at work; he does not feel overly controlled by the organisation and has the freedom to realise objectives in an autonomous way. It has been linked to enhanced creativity, self-esteem, conceptual learning and general well-being.

---

[104]Amabile, TM and SJ Kramer (2010). *What Really Motivates Workers.* Cambridge, MA: HBR Press.
[105]Hackman, JR and EE Lawlor (1971). Employee reactions to job characteristics. *Journal of Applied Psychology*, 55, 259–286.

Intrinsic motivation is associated with increased interest in the task, increased engagement and higher performance due to motivation to feel competent.[106] Internalised extrinsic motivation has been shown to lead to positive outcomes such as well-being, increased productivity and task satisfaction.

Self-determination is supported by participation of the employee in decision making, support for individual initiative, and open communications. In the work environment, the interaction between the manager and the subordinate can be interpreted by the employee in two ways that affect self-determination: as *informational* or *controlling*. Rewards, deadlines and positive feedback are all positive contributors to an employee's self-determination if they are understood by the employee to be informational and not controlling, depending on the style of management. Threats of punishment, surveillance and evaluations tend to be experienced as controlling, and thus negatively affecting the employee's sense of choice, self-esteem, intrinsic motivation and perceived competence.[107]

The theory of self-determination is increasingly important in terms of creating an environment that enables a certain level of autonomy, and empowerment.

An employee who has the freedom to make decisions about how to execute his or her job, and who believes that his work is being performed competently and is having a positive impact on the company, will experience ownership and responsibility for the role, a greater sense of pride, and will be more invested in the organisation. Empirical research has shown that as employees are more empowered their job stress decreases.[108]

One study revealed that those who did not feel in control of their working lives were much more likely to report a sense of powerlessness in their organisation and are much less likely to feel loyal to their organisation or that their organisation was loyal to them. They were also significantly less likely to recommend their organisation as a place to work.[109]

---

[106]Deci, EL *et al.* (1989). Self-determination in a work organization. *Journal of Applied Psychology*, 74(4), 580–590.
[107]Deci, EL *et al.* (1989). Self-determination in a work organization. *Journal of Applied Psychology*, 74(4), 580–590.
[108]Joiner, TA and T Bartram (2004). How empowerment and social support affect Australian nurses' work stressors. *Australian Health Review* 28(1), 56–64.
[109]Work Life Balance Centre (2009). The twenty-four seven work life balance survey.

McClelland's Socially Acquired Needs theory suggests that people with high achievement needs will be particularly motivated by challenging tasks with clearly attainable objectives, timely feedback and more responsibility for innovative assignments.[110]

Studies in organisations have provided support for the propositions that autonomy-supportive (rather than controlling) work environments and managerial methods promote basic need satisfaction, intrinsic motivation and full internalisation of extrinsic motivation, and that these in turn lead to persistence, effective performance, job satisfaction, positive work attitudes, organisational commitment and psychological well-being.[111] Studies have found that managers' autonomy support led to greater satisfaction of the needs for competence, relatedness and autonomy and, in turn, to more job satisfaction, higher performance evaluations, greater persistence, greater acceptance of organisational change and better psychological adjustment.[112]

Best Practices Case Study: GSK

Employee development and empowerment at GSK

British GSK, the fourth largest pharmaceutical company worldwide (99,000 employees in 114 countries), has created programs and structures to empower people and provide opportunities for growth and leadership.[113]

EmpowerMe is an internal source for GSK employees to share ideas, discuss issues and celebrate empowerment. The aim of EmpowerMe is to give employees the tools and inspiration needed to empower teams to make decisions with confidence and accountability. In the last year, more than 150 postings have been shared on the EmpowerMe site.

---

[110]Wiley, C (1997). What motivates employees according to over 40 years of motivation surveys. *International Journal of Manpower,* 18(3), 263–280.

[111]Gagné, M and E Deci (2005). Self-determination theory and work motivation. *Journal of Organizational Behavior*, 26, 331–362.

[112]Gagné, M and E Deci (2005). Self-determination theory and work motivation. *Journal of Organizational Behavior*, 26, 331–362.

[113]GSK Website: http://www.gsk.com/responsibility/our-people.

Mentoring is meant to support and inspire high-performing employees. In 2009 the top three tiers of GSK management made a commitment to mentor at least 1 employee each during 2010. In addition, internal and external *coaching* help accelerate employee development and enhance leadership skills.

GSK provides work-related *training* courses for all employees, in 19 languages in over 100 countries. More than 8,000 of these programmes were offered via the online learning management system. GSK also offers project secondments to help employees learn new skills.

Diverse *committees* provide opportunities for expression and empowerment. CEO Advisory Board is made up of employees from across the company and acts as an informal sounding board for ideas. European Employee Consultation Forum includes employee representatives from 28 EU countries who receive updates and review proposals affecting the structure of the business. UK Information and Consultation (I&C) Forum consists of 15 GSK-elected employee representatives and seven managers and meets three times a year.

'Our goal is for GSK to be recognised as an employer of choice through how we value and empower our people within our workplace culture.'

Development of competencies and progression

Providing opportunities for development is one of the most meaningful ways of demonstrating to an individual that the organisation is willing to invest in him or her; this investment helps to convey the value, raising esteem and in turn fostering the engagement and commitment towards organisational goals. Promotion and growth in the organisation are long-standing factors that motivate people to do their best work. They build challenge and opportunity for achievement into the job itself.

A survey by Development Dimensions International in 2004 interviewed 1,000 staff from companies employing more than 500 workers, and found many to be bored, lacking commitment and looking for a new job. Pay came fifth in the reasons people gave for leaving their jobs. The main reasons were lack of stimulus and no opportunity for advancement (classic Herzberg motivators), 43% left for better promotion chances, 28% for more challenging work; and 23% for a more exciting place to work; and 21% for more varied work (Figure 5.3).

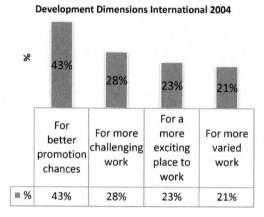

Figure 5.3   Reasons for leaving job (Sample 1,000).

Best Practices Case Study: Sodexo

Sodexo, empowerment and 'social elevator'

With 380,000 employees and 50 million end-users worldwide, Sodexo is the 2nd largest French employer worldwide, 7th largest European employer worldwide and 22nd largest employer worldwide. Although Sodexo has become a large, worldwide company, it remains a 'local' company where *each manager in the field is a true entrepreneur,* close to their clients and *empowered in their decision-making.*

Sodexo characterises the company as a *social elevator that helps people to progress and have a better life.*[114] Ninety-five percent of people who join Sodexo have little education, sometimes no education; training is made available to employees to help them develop or move up the career ladder. In 2009, 30.7% of site managers were promoted to manager grade and 22.8% of employees were promoted to site manager grade.[115]

'If you want your staff to contribute above and beyond the call of duty, you have to give them ownership. This will not happen if all the ideas and decisions are yours... To inspire our staff, we use a number

---

[114]Top 50 companies for diversity (2010). Diversity Inc Magazine; http://www.diversity inc-digital.com/diversityincmedia/201006?pg=96#pg96.
[115]Sodexo Group Human Resources Report (2009).

of strategies. These include involving people in the development of their position, involving them in decision-making and encouraging them to manage up and think outside the box.'

— Stephen Lockley, Managing Director, Sodexo Singapore[116]

People can grow and develop through training and development, progression in task or promotions and opportunities to exert responsibility or to innovate. This contributes to employee motivation and job satisfaction; it also has a direct positive impact on organisations: staff is enabled to operate at a higher level, which makes their organisations more productive and competitive.

Best Practices Case Study: Chemtech

Chemtech, an ambitious strategy for career growth and development opportunities

Chemtech, a Brazilian leader in information technology, 1100 employees in 2010, has been repeatedly named among the 'Best Companies to Work for' in Brazil and Latin America (2007, 2008, 2009, 2010). Chemtech set up an ambitious strategy for career growth and development opportunities. Three programs have been developed specifically:

Mentoring: 'Programa de Desenvolvimento Interno'[117]

This internal development program aims at combining the know-how of more experienced professionals with the enthusiasm of newly recruited talents.

Promotion and Careers: 'Carreira em Y'[118]

Chemtech wants to offer flexible career and growth opportunities within the company. They allow and encourage internal rotation and believe that 'each person has something special to offer.' 'Career in Y' gives employees the opportunity to develop either a management or technical career. The choice of this career either technical or managerial is based on the professional's choice and on an evaluation of individual performances.

---

[116] *Business Times*, September 2009.
[117] Hr.com.br, May 2010.
[118] Hr.com.br, November 2008.

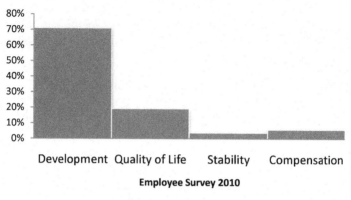

Figure 5.4   Chemtech: What employees value most.

'The idea is to provide career options for engineers, technical and management, ensuring the same wage conditions,' says Romão Daniella Gallo, the company's HR manager.

Training[119]

The Chemtech Corporate University (UCC) was created to support the development of the employees and encourage the Chemtech co-workers to keep on improving.

Chemtech provides MBA and in-company Master's degree courses in partnership with first-class educational institutions such as the Fluminense Federal University (UFF) and the Federal University of Rio de Janeiro (UFRJ). The UCC also supplies several internal courses provided by Chemtech's professionals to share the company's knowledge in different areas of activity.

Organisations can encourage responsibility and leadership opportunities through involving employees in continuous efficiency improvement; creating an environment where innovators have freedom to experiment, fail and try again; and allowing employees to test drive a new role.

Training and learning development includes aspects such as skills and knowledge, attitude and behavior, leadership and determination as well as ethics and morality. There are many different training and development methods such as training, coaching and mentoring according to individual

---

[119]Chemtech Website; http://www.chemtech.com.br/lportal/web/guest/universidade_corporativa.

training needs and organisational training needs. Good management can also help people to unlock their potential.

5.5.2. *Incentive and Recognition*

> *'People may take a job for more money, but they often leave it for more recognition.'*
>
> *Bob Nelson*

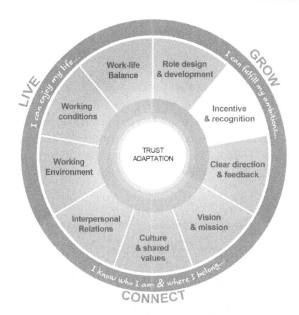

Incentive and recognition systems play a key role in stimulating motivation by acknowledging and rewarding exemplary performance. They play a critical role in drawing attention to organisational values and desired behaviours, in driving employee motivation towards good performance, and in fostering loyalty and commitment. An effective motivation program will benefit from the concerted effect of both recognition and incentives when they are carefully designed, implemented and managed.

Definition of Incentive:

Incentive refers to the motivational practice of stimulating a desired employee performance through the use of rewards that are linked to specific performance goals.

Definition of Recognition:

Recognition is an after-the-fact appreciation or acknowledgement of some-one's behaviour, actions or business result that supports the organisation's goals and values. Recognition can be formal or informal.

Incentive and recognition are two complementary factors that can be leveraged for fostering both short-term and long-term motivation. It should be used to motivate all workers to improve the quality of their performance, and also to reward top performers.[120]

Incentive

Incentive refers to the motivational practice of stimulating a desired employee performance through the use of rewards that are linked to specific performance goals. The reward represents an incentive value for the employee that stimulates action towards a specific outcome. Rewards are not intended to be coercive or manipulative; they simply provide an employee with a means to satisfy a desire and to attach a value to the performance outcome.

Spotlight on the Theory: Expectancy Value Theory

Victor Vroom (1964); Porter and Lawlor (1968)

When faced with a task in work people will make choices on which task to complete and how much effort to exert based on expectancies and values of the situation. People will not have the same motivation for each task.

Expectancy theory focuses on the process that translates needs into action and produces a certain outcome. According to Vroom, when people choose what behavior to pursue at work, they evaluate the task in relation to their needs and they take into account three main factors that influence the choice of task and the effort they exert.

Expectancy: Will my effort result in the accomplishment of the expected task? What am I able to achieve? The person's perception of his abilities and confidence is key for motivation.

---

[120]An executive white paper based on the study authored by Harold D. Stolovitch, Richard E. Clark and Steven J. Condly. Sponsored by the International Society for Performance Improvement, with a grant from The Incentive Research Foundation.

Instrumentality: Will the completion of the task bring about satisfaction of personal desires? What am I going to obtain from completion? Effort is a means to obtain a reward linked to a need: need for achievement, need for esteem and progression.

Valence: How much do I value the expected outcome of the task? The higher the value the individual places on the outcome, the more motivated he will be.

Organisations should be familiar with the differences in employee values in rewards (tangible or intangible including self-esteem or appreciation from peers) through evaluations.

They should also ensure that professional goals are likely to provide satisfaction to the worker: Does the worker associate the completion of tasks with outcomes he personally values? Can his interest in the task be increased by adding value to success? Is the worker confident in his ability to perform?

In addition, communication and feedback should not be overlooked both regarding desirable performance and linking rewards to outcomes.

Zoom on . . . The Conditions under Which Incentives Work Best

Incentive Research Foundation

— When current performance is inadequate: *to stimulate* better standards of *performance*
— If the cause of the inadequate performance is related to deficiencies in *motivation*
— If the desired performance type and level can be quantified
— When the *goal is challenging but achievable*
— When the focus on promoting a particular behavior does not conflict with everyday goals.

Incentives have had their fair share of critics over the years, mainly due to their misuse and abuse. When Frederick Taylor introduced the practice of scientific management in the earlier part of the 20th century, workers were enticed into higher levels of productivity through the promise of incentives. Each incremental increase in productivity was tied to a specific reward.

Today incentives, when used appropriately, can play a positive role in motivating employees.

---

[121]An executive white paper based on the study authored by Harold D. Stolovitch, Richard E. Clark and Steven J. Condly. Sponsored by the International Society for Performance Improvement, with a grant from The Incentive Research Foundation.

Fair management

— A reward program needs to be *fairly and transparently implemented* for it to be effective. Research by Jobpartners in 2006 found that *79% of employees feel their organisation's rewards system is not fair and 64% of their employees feel undervalued.*

— *Measurement is key* both to assess the results compared to the goals, and also to give visibility during the programs. Today's Web-based incentive program technology makes it possible to get almost real-time performance data so that people can adjust efforts accordingly.

Best Practices Case Study: Awards in Google

Research shows that *awards play a key role in communication* because they help get attention and convey the organisation's commitment to achieving its goals.[122] In Google, the awards given to staff generally reflect the importance of innovation and teamwork: two goals that Google believes are instrumental to success.

The Founders' Award → Recognition Program

Awarded to employees or teams for an achievement that has created significant value for Google

In 2005, Google awarded approximately $45 million in restricted stocks to employees working on 11 different projects.[123]

Recognition

Recognition is the practice of acknowledging or giving special attention to employee action, effort, behavior or performance that supports the organisation's goals and values.[124] In general, recognition is not connected to predetermined goals or performance levels, but instead is used to

---

[122] An executive white paper based on the study authored by Harold D. Stolovitch, Richard E. Clark, and Steven J. Condly. Sponsored by the International Society for Performance Improvement, with a grant from The Incentive Research Foundation.

[123] Hafner, K (2005). New incentive for Google employees: Awards worth millions; http://query.nytimes.com/gst/fullpage.html?res=9B06EFDD123BF932A35751C0A9639C8B63.

[124] Human Capital Institute (2009). The value and ROI in employee recognition. HCI White Paper.

reinforce desired behaviours by providing the individual with an indication of what the organisation values as exemplary behavior.

Recognition acknowledges behaviours that are linked to organisational culture, job performance and business value after the behaviours are expressed. Recognition programs aim to increase both employee motivation and engagement so employees will sustain and increase the behaviours linked to good job performance. In particular, recognition is most effectively used if only employed to acknowledge extraordinary accomplishments or outstanding behaviour. It can lose meaning and become a negative lever if used too often and for mediocre behavior. The writer Mark Twain highlighted this 'great law of human action', when he stated that 'in order to make a man or a boy covet a thing, it is only necessary to make the thing difficult to obtain.'[125] Recognition is also valued higher when given by someone that the employee holds in high esteem such as a manager or a special thanks from the CEO.

Spotlight on the Theory: Recognition

Many theorists have identified recognition as having very powerful motivational value.

Herzberg, in his two-factor theory, found that recognition was one of the factors that most strongly impacted an employee's motivation, second only to achievement.

Deci noted that if recognition provides people with positive information about their self-competence, then it will support *intrinsic motivation.* The need for competence is an important intrinsic psychological need.

Recognition contributes to the esteem need, which is one of the higher-order psychological needs depicted in *Maslow's hierarchy of needs* pyramid.

Recognition seems to be among the best (and certainly most cost-effective) methods of improving work motivation and employee engagement.[126]

The need for approval and appreciation is a fundamental need for human beings, and very powerful within each one of us because it tells

---

[125]Mark Twain (1876). *The Adventures of Tom Sawyer.*
[126]Human Capital Institute (2009). The value and ROI in employee recognition. Also see the Kanungo and Mendonca, and Gallup studies.

us that what we have done is right and worthy of notice. Human beings are programmed to seek approval from their very first days of life and thus in work situations the intrinsic psychological need for appreciation is very important.[127] The biggest performance gains come when people become emotionally engaged. Recognition and, with careful consideration, incentive awards should have a positive impact on emotion and organisational spirit. Positive feedback is therefore an integral part of a well-designed recognition program. Recognition is most effective when given immediately after the accomplishment or desired behaviour.

Recognition is also one of the most used methods for motivation. It is found by managers to be widely effective and in most corporate cultures. Yet, it is important to match the form of recognition to the situation or person. In certain cultures award ceremonies or 'Employee of the Month' may be disliked by people.

Spotlight on the Theory: Reinforcement Theory

B.F. Skinner (1957)

In the organisation desirable behaviours can be encouraged by linking those behaviours with positive consequences

Reinforcement theory, like expectancy theory, suggests that in any given situation people will explore a variety of possible behaviours and make choices when deciding to pursue one course of action or task over another. These choices are affected by *the consequences of earlier behaviours*. It assumes that people explore different behaviours and choose those that result in the most desirable outcomes. The consequences of behaviour are called reinforcement.

A manager can reinforce desired behaviours through recognition. For instance, an employee displaying friendly service could be commended on this behaviour. This has a dual purpose: first the employee understands that friendly service is a desired form of performance; and second it supports an employee's desire for esteem.

It is important to note that negative reinforcement is not advisable: an employee's esteem and engagement could be eroded through repeated reprimand or criticism. Feedback on an employee's limits or failings should be approached constructively and positively.

---

[127]The Forum for People Performance Management and Measurement (2005). Match Employee Awards to Specific Organizational Objectives for Optimal Success.

Zoom on... Effective Recognition

Recognition Professionals International[128]

Day-to-day recognition encompasses a wide range of acknowledgement that is frequent, ongoing and informal. It may consist of intangible recognition, awards, celebrations or eligibility for awards or celebrations to recognise behaviours that support organisational goals and values. It may include thank you notes or forms that employees give to one another or verbal praise. All employees can participate in this recognition, supporting recognition up, down and across the organisation.

Informal recognition singles out individuals or teams for progress towards milestones, achieving goals or projects completed. Celebrations may include low-cost mementos or refreshments as a way to celebrate achievements or outstanding positive behavior. It is less structured than formal recognition and reaches a larger percentage of the employee population.

Formal recognition consists of a structured program with defined processes and criteria linked to organisational values and goals, a nomination and selection process and an awards ceremony where employees receive public recognition and are presented with awards in a formal setting. Generally speaking, it is an annual program and only a small percentage of employees are recognised.

Best Practices Case Study: Southwest Airlines

Recognition in Southwest Airlines

Kick-Tail Peer Recognition

Southwest Airlines have a process of peer recognition, called 'Kick-Tail' recognition, which is used widely throughout the 30,000 employees in the company. The principle is that special 'Kick-Tail' postcards are available to employees, customers and every time they see an employee doing an exceptionally good job, or providing extraordinary service, any time they

---

[128] Recognition Professionals International (2007). Scotiabank — realigning employee recognition to business strategy reaps measurable rewards. White Paper, Best Practice and Best in Class Recipient, Recognition Professionals International.

think a fellow employee deserves a pat on the back, they fill out a Kick-Tail card and give it to the person who then turns in the card and is eligible for a prize draw. There is a budget of $1 million for these prizes each year in Southwest.[129]

The value of incentives and recognition for the employer

The combined action of incentives and recognition can be used to create a positive cycle of ever-increasing employee engagement and motivation, with resulting improvements in job performance, provided that they are adapted to the person, the circumstances and the objective. It is important to note that incentive and recognition programs should include multiple forms of rewards or awards to suit the person and the situation.

Best Practices Case Study: Recognition in McDonalds

McDonald's, the leading global food service retailer, places emphasis on employee recognition through corporate awards. McDonald's acknowledge that they face a steep challenge to retain workers in an industry that is widely known for a high level of turnover. McDonald's has the added challenge of upturning negative associations with the term 'McJob' as well as offering consistently good service in a company with a large number of franchises. Recognising employees for their efforts by offering awards forms an important part of their approach to boost motivation in the long-term.

At global level:

General awards are the following: Corporate Service Award Program, Team Awards, Bright Idea Awards, Budget Sub Committee Award, Government Relations Award, Drive Thru Award, Employee of the Month Plaques[130]

---

[129] Interview with Ginger Hardage, VP Culture and Communications, Southwest Airlines, 30 August 2010.
[130] JTH Recognition: McDonald's Corporation; http://jthemployeerecognitionprograms. com/index.php?option=com_content&task=view&id=38&Itemid=9.

McDonald's President's Award, the highest McDonald's award, recognises the top 1% of employees who achieve considerable results in strategic initiatives.[131]

Circle of Excellence Award is given to top teams worldwide to recognise their contributions for advancing McDonald's vision.

Operators Network Recognition Award recognises one's active role in women's leadership.

Examples at local level:

United States: *Ray Kroc Awards* is the annual performance-based recognition of the top performing McDonald's restaurant managers in the country. It consists of a cash award, a Ray Kroc Award trophy and pin, and a trip to Chicago for the awards gala.[132]

Australia: *Outstanding Restaurant Managers Award* is an award for employees who represent the image of a complete professional, an outstanding manager who takes pride in their work and in McDonald's.[133]

England: *Three-Legged Stool Award* recognises the leadership and team-playing abilities of a restaurant manager that have seen his business set a national benchmark for UK franchisees.[134]

Canada: *Golden Maple Leaf Awards* rewards exceptional performance. The best employees in their field are awarded up to $10,000 in post-secondary education scholarships.[135]

---

[131]Mead, J and P Werhane (2008). *Started as Crew A*. Charlottesville, VA: Darden Business Publishing.
[132]*PR Newswire*, March 2010.
[133]*Northern Miner*, January 2010.
[134]*Birmingham Post*, December 2008.
[135]*National Post*, December 2008.

5.5.3.   *Clear Direction and Feedback*

> *'People with goals succeed because they know where they are going; it's as simple as that.'*
>
> Earl Nightingale

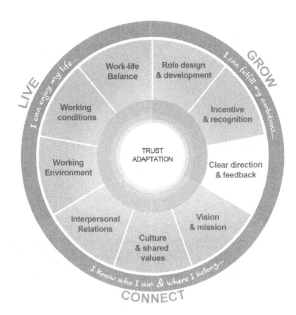

Clear and challenging goals represent an effective lever for driving employees to perform to high standards and infusing work tasks with a greater sense of purpose and significance. Combining clear goals with feedback helps employees to evaluate their performance and learn. Employees perform better and feel more valuable when they know what is expected of them.

Definition of Clear Direction and Feedback:

Clear direction refers to the process of setting specific goals and helping employees work towards the objective. Goal-setting ideally involves establishing specific objectives that are challenging but attainable, incorporating deadlines and quantifiable measures, and providing feedback during the task and after its completion to enable people to measure and adapt their behaviour.

Setting goals

By defining the purpose of a task and tying it to a desirable end result, effective leaders infuse work with meaning and purpose. The task remains the same, but the significance of the task in employees' minds is raised considerably. Effective managers help to connect the individual's goals with the company's goals. This not only helps employees to feel that their work is purposeful and has an impact on company success; it also ensures that the employee can prioritise tasks in terms of importance to company performance.

Spotlight on the Theory: Goal-setting Theory

Edwin Locke and Gary Latham (1980)

Edwin Locke and Gary Latham have produced a compelling stream of research over the past 35 years demonstrating that difficult, specific goals lead to better task performance.

According to Locke *et al.* (1981), a review of both laboratory and field studies on the effects of setting goals when performing a task found that *in 90% of the studies, specific and challenging goals lead to higher performance* than easy goals, 'do your best' goals or no goals.[136]

The Corporate Leadership Council Study (2005)[137] highlights the importance of effective goal-setting through a focus on the strengths of the individual, accompanied with constructive discussion on suggestions for improvement, and long-term career prospects, rather than on weaknesses. Focusing on strengths reinforces performance-enhancing behaviour and promotes a stronger identification with the work. A positive system of performance review can have an impact of up the 36%; a performance review that place a strong emphasis on weaknesses can have a negative impact of up to 27% on performance.

---

[136]Locke, EA, KN Shaw, LM Saari and GP Latham (1981). Goal setting and task performance: 1969–1980. *Psychological Bulletin*, 90(1), 125–152.

[137]Corporate Leadership Council (2005). *Managing for High Performance and Retention*. Washington, D.C.: Corporate Leadership Council.

Spotlight on the Theory: Self-efficacy

Alfred Bandura (1963)

Orator and philosopher Norman Vincent Peale, author of *The Power of Positive Thinking*, once contended that 'any fact facing us is not as important as our attitude towards it, for that determines our success or failure'.[138]

Self-efficacy refers to the belief that one has the capabilities to execute the courses of actions required to successfully perform the goal task. It relates to both inherent personal beliefs regarding ability, and also past experiences relating to mastery of a task.

People with high self-efficacy set higher goals than do people with lower self-efficacy, are more committed to assigned goals, find and use better task strategies to attain the goals and respond more positively to negative feedback than do people with low self-efficacy.

Studies have found that individuals do not typically give their maximum effort when they are simply instructed to do their best. Specific goals are best attained when quantitative measures are set and a specific deadline for attaining the goal is added. This is because specific goals define what constitutes an effective level of performance and individuals do not tend to give their maximum effort if they are simply told to 'do their best'.[139]

> *'On days when workers have the sense they're making headway in their jobs, or when they receive support that helps them overcome obstacles, their emotions are most positive and their drive to succeed is at its peak.'*
>
> *Teresa Amabile*

Setting sub-goals, particularly in the case of difficult goals, has also been proven as effective. Mini-goals or sub-goals provide clear markers of progress and reduce the risk of demoralisation or loss of motivation during the progress towards accomplishment of the goal.

---

[138] Wiedenkeller, K (2010). SVP, Human Resources, AMC Entertainment in 'Some like it hot? Work environments impact productivity', *Film Journal International*, 4 May 2010; http://www.filmjournal.com/filmjournal/content_display/columns-and-blogs/the-people-factor/e3i7b2c50df9c8f86ff8be25b86bc20bd72.

[139] Seijts, G (2001). Setting goals when performance doesn't matter. *Ivey Business Journal*, January/February 2001.

Setting goals helps people to reach a target, to stretch and challenge a person to accomplish a task; but allowing people a certain amount of freedom or volition in *how* they complete the task can have a powerful impact on the quality of the task completed. As Teresa Amabile notes, people tend to be more creative 'if you give them freedom to decide how to climb a particular mountain. You needn't let them choose which mountain to climb. In fact, clearly specified strategic goals often enhance people's creativity.' This autonomy and freedom to complete a task as one sees fit can help to create task ownership, self-determination and thus intrinsic motivation (Figure 5.5).[140]

Having precise, defined goals helps us to complete tasks; according to the psychologist Peter Gollwitzer 'pre-deciding should help a person protect goal pursuit from tempting distractions, bad habits, or competing goals'.[141]

Having a goal stimulates the individual to develop specific strategies to reach the goal target. In other words, people can be motivated to think outside the box in order to meet an ambitious goal. Goals can play an important role in helping employees to progress on a daily basis, and serve as a valuable marker of improvement and advancement. Similar to the idea of 'small wins', a study conducted by Teresa Amabile examined the effect of emotions on motivation, and found that one of the most contingent factors on the satisfaction of the employee is the feeling that they have made progress in their work on a day to day basis. The study on peoples'

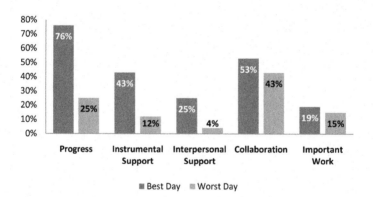

Figure 5.5   What happens on a great day.

---

[140]Amabile, T (1998). How to kill creativity. *Harvard Business Review*, September, 77–87.

[141]Gollwitzer, P (1999). Implementation intentions. *American Psychologist*, 54, 493–503.

feelings towards their work revealed that the feeling that one has progressed in a task was noted on 76% of people's 'best days', when their reported moods were most buoyant, and on only 25% of their 'worst'. By providing clear goals and supporting the employee in the achievement of these goals through resources and encouragement, managers have a powerful influence over the circumstances that facilitate progress.[142]

Zoom on ... Small Wins

Albert Banduras conducted research on the effects of goal-setting on dieters and found that those who set a series of mini goals lost more weight than individuals who set one long-term goal alone. Setting sub-goals in conjunction with a chief goal enhanced an individual's confidence. A series of small goals allows the person to achieve many 'small wins'[143] that has a positive effect on self-efficacy and thus facilitate the achievement of the longer term goal.[144]

Best Practices Case Study: GlaxoSmithKline

Performance and development planning

PDP is the basis for establishing personal goals and means at GSK. The PDP process also encompasses development planning and a review of progress throughout the year against objectives, behaviours and development. The process also aims to align individual contributions with GSK's business goals; appraisals impact on reward and future career development.

360-degree feedback: The assessments are structured around GSK's values and behaviours, and help managers to reflect on how others perceive them and to improve relationships within and outside the company.[145]

---

[142]Amabile, TM and SJ Kramer (2010). What really motivates workers. *Harvard Business Review*, 88(1), 44–45.

[143]The concept of 'small wins' was developed by Karl Weick.

[144]Seijts, G (2001). Setting goals when performance doesn't matter. *Ivey Business Journal*, January/February 2001.

[145]GSK Website; http://www.gsk.com/responsibility/our-people/developing-our-people.htm.

Feedback

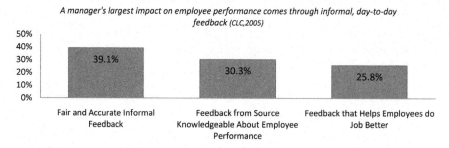

Figure 5.6   Delivering feedback: Percentage of impact on performance.

An important aspect of goal setting is the feedback that the leader issues following the task, providing employees with a yardstick to measure their behaviour. Good goal-setting should be allied with recognition and reward for good performance. Combining clear goals with a two-way feedback should be used to ensure that people have the resources and skills to reach a goal. Informal feedback is one of the most powerful drivers managers have to improve employee performance (Figure 5.6).

According to CLC research, based on extensive analysis of data from more than 90,000 employees in 135 organisations from around the world, fair and accurate feedback can boost employee engagement by up to 40% and discretionary effort by up to 23.3%.[146] While an emphasis on employee weaknesses can lead to diminished engagement and satisfaction, employees will respond to feedback that is specific and helps to guide improvement.[147]

Performance reviews

Performance reviews can represent an ideal forum for a positive discussion on both the employee's long-term career prospects, and a constructive conversation with suggestions for improving performance, or a look at what skills and behaviours the employee will need to achieve future goals. A practical, specific discussion will demonstrate the commitment of the manager to the employee's success, encourage individual self-efficacy and build engagement (Figure 5.7).

---

[146]Corporate Leadership Council (2005). *Managing for High Performance and Retention*. Washington, D.C.: Corporate Leadership Council.
[147]Corporate Leadership Council (2005). *Managing for High Performance and Retention*. Washington, D.C.: Corporate Leadership Council.

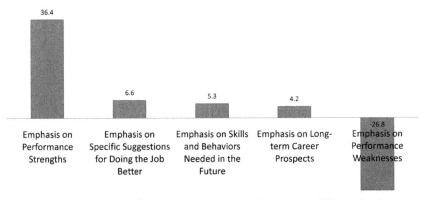

Source: CLC (2005) Managing for High Performance and Retention.

Figure 5.7   Performance reviews: Percentage of impacts on performance.

5.6.   Connect: I Know Who I Am and Where I Belong...

As human beings, we have an innate need for interpersonal relations. In quality of life studies, relationships with family and friends are recurrently identified as one of the most important determinants of well-being. 'Love, family, community — those are supposed to be the true sources of happiness, while work simply gives us the means to enjoy them'.[148] Maslow identified belongingness, love or relationships as a fundamental human need. Herzberg found that personal relationships was an important hygiene need for people in the workplace; when relations with co-workers is poor, the negative impact on overall satisfaction at work can be significant and is therefore an important factor for individual well-being.[149] People by nature seek to forge bonds and with others near them. Today people spend more time at work and by necessity build this connection with people in the workplace.[150] Finding a meaning from work and an identity with the organisation is an important factor of motivation at work and for fostering a greater engagement to the organisation. Employees that feel like an important and integral part of the company strategy tend to be more motivated to contribute in a positive way to company success. Fostering connection in the workplace can be leveraged through the levers of *Vision & Mission, Culture & Shared Values,* and *Interpersonal Relationships.*

---

[148]Work: Thank God it's Monday (9 January 2005). *Time.*
[149]Herzberg, F (1987). One more time — How do you motivate employees? *Harvard Business Review,* 65(5), 109–112.
[150]Along with benefits and pay, employees seek friends on the job (20 February 2002). *Wall Street Journal.*

5.6.1.   *Vision and Mission*

'*To enlist people in a vision, leaders must know their con-
stituents as well as their cultures and languages. It is not
just connecting different sets of people into one, but rather
connecting people with a shared vision who have a strong
relationship with each other.*'

Frank Mulhern

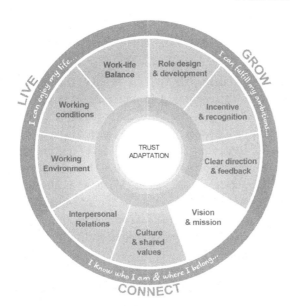

The connection that employees feel with the organisation influences their
commitment and willingness to strive collectively for achieving company's
objectives. The execution of vision and mission is strong when people
understand the objectives of the company, know where the organisation
is headed and feel an important part of it. When employees feel a sense of
ownership and connection with the company, and when they care about the
future of the organisation, they become more invested in their individual
roles and the company's performance.

Definition of Vision and Mission:

A company's core purpose is that all employees, activities and processes
collectively contribute to the achievement of organisational goals. Vision
can be defined as the long-term view of what an organisation is striving
to become. The mission of the company articulates the vision and sets a
roadmap for the future.

A vision reflects a firm's fundamental beliefs, experiences, shared values, future goals and opportunities.[151] Pratt and Ashforth (2003) indicate the importance of establishing a vision that relates to the meaningfulness of work to employees.[152] A clearly articulated vision leads to developing a mission demonstrating commitment and inspiring a sense of direction to the members of the organisation.[153]

Strategic direction

Inspiring and guiding people, connecting employee goals to the strategic vision

Helping employees to connect with the vision and the mission of the organisation can be difficult to achieve. A framed mission statement hanging on the wall will not create the connection that is needed for employees to really know where they are headed in the organisation, feel a part of it and willingly contribute to it, that is, to feel a sense of motivation to strive towards organisational goals. Kotter (1995) argues that the primary source of failed leadership is uncertainty of vision. Without a clear and strong vision, a leader's strategy can become a jumble of confusing and conflicting tasks that can take the organisation in the wrong direction, or no direction at all. Thus, providing a strong vision is the first and most important step in organisational leadership.[154]

When employees subscribe to the vision of the company, understand its objectives and believe they play a role in achieving them, they become more invested in their individual job and the company's success. First, they are more likely to derive satisfaction from their work as it makes it meaningful, and they tend to approach their job with a sense of pride. Second, striving towards a well-defined and challenging goal contributes to creating the energy necessary to achieve high performance and quality of service, especially when people feel inspired by organisational vision.

Leaders and managers need to link the organisation's vision and values to the employees' day-to-day work. They should communicate the vision continuously to ensure that there is no uncertainty about the direction a

---

[151]Kouzes, JM and BZ Posner (2002). *The Leadership Challenge: How to Keep Getting Extraordinary Things Done in Organizations.* San Francisco, CA: Jossey-Bass.

[152]Pratt, MG and BE Ashforth (2003). Fostering meaningfulness in work and at work. In *Positive Organizational Scholarship: Foundations of a New Discipline*, KS Cameron, JE Dutton and RE Quinn (eds.), pp. 309–327. San Francisco, CA: Berrett-Koehler Publishers.

[153]Kotter, JP (1995). Leading change: Why transformation efforts fail. *Harvard Business Review*, 73(2), 59–67.

[154]Kotter, JP (1995). Leading change: Why transformation efforts fail. *Harvard Business Review*, 73(2), 59–67.

team is heading. They should help them see how the work they do every day connects to the bigger picture for people to be able to believe in the importance of their work.

Zoom on... Connecting with the Organisation

Connecting with the identity of the organisation because of the organisation's image, notoriety or purpose can be a motivating factor for many people. Would you rather work at Google or Yahoo?

In *Motivation: What Keeps You Going Besides Coffee*, Mark Jaffe asks, 'What level of eminence, reputation and public esteem does your company enjoy? For example, would you rather be a SVP at Wal-Mart or a VP at Nordstrom? Everything else being equal, that is'.[155]

Feeling a connection and a sense of pride for a company may have a bearing on a person's attitude towards the organisation and their willingness to strive for greater performance and organisational success.

Vision and employee engagement

Having a strong connection with the organisation is an important determinant of engagement. Gibbons offers a definition of engagement as: 'A heightened emotional connection that an employee feels for his or her organisation, that influences him or her to exert greater discretionary effort to his or her work'.[156] It can also be described as the 'collective movement towards the company and individual objectives', thus implying a sense of cohesiveness between employee and organisational objectives. Without good connection with the organisational vision, employee vision could very well be running in a different direction to that of the organisation. Equally, an organisation that fails to incorporate employee well-being in the vision of the organisation will have difficulty developing a vision that inspires the employees.[157] This is demonstrated with companies such as Southwest Airlines: 'Our focus as a company has to be on our employees, because if our employees are not happy, our customers aren't going to get decent service'.[158]

---

[155] Mark Jaffe (2010). Motivation: What keeps you going besides coffee; http://www.bnet.com/blog/executive-recruiting/motivation-what-keeps-you-going-besides-coffee/152.

[156] Gibbons, J (2006). Employee engagement: A review current research and its implications, *The Conference Board*.

[157] Won-joo, Yun and F Mulhern (2009). Leadership and the performance of people in organizations: Enriching employees and connecting people, *Forum for People Performance Management and Measurement Publication*, November.

[158] Business Matters (1998). *Customer Service*. New York: Harper Collins.

Leadership

Leaders develop and share corporate vision; they also play a key role in translating values into reality and sustaining them through a strong culture. The role of leadership is to unite the people in the organisation into a meaningful 'community' that employees like to identify with and take pride in belonging to.[159]

Good leaders offer a clear vision that is both coherent and credible and sustained by a set of values to inspire people to follow suit. This is the reason the personality of founders usually has a deep impact on organisations, and a founder's values and character traits can permeate the culture.

In a 2010 press release, John Larrere, India national director of Hay Group's Leadership and Talent Practice, and co-leader of the Best Companies for Leadership Study conducted by Bloomberg BusinessWeek.com and the Hay Group, stated: 'For organisations to succeed, they will need to understand what key leadership elements are paramount in driving their organisations towards growth. It's more than just getting people to produce the right outcomes. It's about getting them to be passionate about their work and grooming them to handle the challenges ahead. The Best Companies for Leadership have figured this out'.[160]

Spotlight on the Theory: Communication and Job Enrichment

Frederick Herzberg (1969)

Connecting with the leaders

Herzberg's theory of job enrichment put forth the idea that having a direct communication link between the upper echelons of the organisational hierarchy with the lower levers was an important factor of job enrichment and the value that an employee could take from the role. When barriers are created that hamper the channels of communication in the organisation, the individual employee can feel unconnected with the vision and strategy of the organisation.

---

[159]Minztberg, H (2009). Rebuilding companies as communities. *Harvard Business Review*, July–August, pp. 140–143.

[160]Motivation in Today's Workplace: The Link to Performance, Society for Human Resources Management (SHRM) India; http://www.shrmindia.org/motivation-today%E2%80%99s-workplace-link-performance.

Best Practices Case Study: HCL

HCL: making employees a proactive part of the company vision[161]

HCL is an Indian PC manufacturer and IT services provider that built its success on an innovative *employee-centric* culture.

In 2005, when Vineet Nayar took over as president, HCL adopted a radical approach to employee transformation that would disrupt hierarchical command-and-control organisations. At that time they had an attrition rate of 17% (much higher than competitors), and a 'demoralised workforce'. Five years later, HCL has become India's largest PC maker, it is one of India's fastest growing IT services companies and its revenue has tripled.

The human resources strategy, called 'Employee First, Customer Second', is based on the philosophy that delighted employees translate customers into delighted ones, and therefore the needs of the employees are placed *before* the needs of the customers. The aim is to create a unique employee organisation, drive an inverted organisational structure, create transparency and accountability within the organisation and encourage a value-driven culture.

Results of EFCS Strategy proved as follows: increased employee engagement, enhanced customer experience, improved financial performance, attracting the best, lower employee turnover, positive working environment, positive company image, higher productivity and performance.

'It's about creating a new kind of corporation. It's about empowering extra-ordinary individuals'.[162]

---

[161] University of Virginia case on HCL; http://www.hcltech.com/pdf/Darden.pdf.
[162] HCL website; http://www.hcltech.com/employee-first/.

5.6.2. *Culture and Shared Values*

> '*A company without a compelling culture is like a person without a personality — flesh and bones but no life force, no soul.*'
>
> Henry Mintzberg

You encounter the culture of an organisation as you enter; it is an internal philosophy or set of shared values that influence how people within the organisation treat each other and treat clients. People want to work with others who share the same values and have a common understanding of what the company is about. People feel valued when they are part of something that reflects their values and a positive culture thus infuses people with a sense of common and collaborative purpose.

Definition of Culture and Shared Values:

Culture can be defined as the general pattern of mindsets, beliefs and values that the members of the organisation share in common. The shared values are lived by the people in the organisation on a daily basis. Shared values link the organisation together; and the culture inspires people and nurtures an attitude of relentless growth.

Organisational culture is an understood code of behaviour unique to the organisation that guides how members of the organisation think, feel and act within the framework of that organisation. Most importantly, according to MIT's Edgar Schein, a leading scholar in organisational culture, the essence of culture lies in the fact that it is a product of common experiences of successfully addressing internal and external problems. The common experiences shared by a particular group when working together to overcome challenges leads to the formation of a set of basic assumptions that will shape and influence how this group solve problems, work together and view the world. Schein asserts that culture is only found where there is a definable group with a significant history of togetherness. It is widely acknowledged that organisational cultures have an impact upon motivation and company performance.[163] It can therefore be a powerful motivational lever for organisational effectiveness.

Identity and cohesion

Corporate culture reflects the organisation: it should be emphasised that culture is not a 'part' of an organisation but rather its embodiment.[164] Therefore an effective culture is partly built on other key motivators and reinforces them. For instance, successful organisations often have a corporate culture that values achievement, empowerment, recognition, and that links to a shared mission. Culture also provides good means to communicate on those shared organisational values.

The importance today of cohesiveness amongst people in the organisation has been highlighted by many authors. Frank Mulhern of Northwestern University refers to this as the 'human value connection'. This represents what Mulhern refers to as a 'flow of performance'; organisations succeed because information and actions flow from person to person. Henry Mintzberg notes that 'a company without a compelling culture is like a person without a personality — flesh and bones but no life force, no soul'.[165] Mintzberg has asserted the need for companies to foster a sense of 'communityship' within the organisation, for companies to rebuild themselves into places of engagement, where people are committed to one another and their organisation.[166]

Fostering this sense of 'communityship', according to Minztberg, means 'caring about our work, our colleagues, and our place in the world', and in

---

[163] Denison (1990). *Corporate Culture and Organizational Effectiveness*. New York: John Wiley & Sons.

[164] Smircich, L (1983). Concepts of culture and organizational analysis. *Administrative Science Quarterly*, 28, 339–358.

[165] Minztberg, H (2009). Rebuilding companies as communities. *Harvard Business Review*, July–August, pp. 140–143.

[166] Minztberg, H (2009). Rebuilding companies as communities. *Harvard Business Review*, July–August, pp. 140–143.

turn being inspired by this caring. Southwest Airlines is an example of a company that has fostered strong values in the organisation and has built the culture on these values.

Best Practices Case Study: Southwest Airlines[167]

An inimitable culture: Treat others as you would like to be treated yourself

'Our culture is the sum of our people, and each of us must continue to own it!'

A strong culture of caring is palpable in Southwest; employees share the common value of treating others as you would like to be treated yourself. This value is perpetuated within the company and it is also the driving value in how employees treat the customer. Colleen Barrett, president emeritus, underlines the impact of this value: 'We trust that the goodness of our people will pay off in spades — for each other, for customers, and, ultimately, for our stockholders.'

This value reinforces morale in the organisation, as well as motivating people to treat customers well and deliver excellent customer service. Colleen Barrett believes that this is an important motivation for people to stay with the organisation: 'They [employees] stay here because they are making a difference every day, and they feel good about what they are doing. Our lives revolve around Southwest and its culture, and that's just how we like it.'

According to Southwest, 'Culture is using your lunch break to help plan your Christmas party; it's organising a burger burn to raise funds for an employee in need; it's cooking at the Ronald McDonald House after you've worked an eight hour shift....'

Organisational citizenship

Many employees want to connect with something bigger and more significant than the organisation and their daily working lives. In one survey, it was revealed that 77% of people indicated a company's commitment to social causes influenced their decision about where to work.[168] Companies who are socially responsible were found to have more than a 10% higher

---

[167]Wiersema, F (1998). Customer Service, Business Masters.
[168]Burud, S and M Tumolo (2004). *Leveraging the New Human Capital.* Palo Alto, CA: Davies-Black Publishing.

sales growth, profit growth and return on equity than companies who are not on the list. Fortune 500 companies with a good reputation are actually more profitable and stock prices were relatively higher among 216 companies known for being socially responsible.[169]

Best Practices Case Study: Opportunities for Citizenship

... at GSK[170]

Orange Day allows employees to take one day per year, fully paid, to volunteer for a chosen community project that they support. Not only does the employee benefit from the team building experience but the organization receives help with projects at no cost.

Lasting for a period of 3 to 6 months, a PULSE volunteer will work full-time with one of GSK's partner NGO to make a significant impact in impoverished communities around the world. Employees continue to receive their GSK salary during the placement. In 2009, 58 PULSE volunteers did assignments with 25 NGOs in 18 countries, representing an in-kind donation of £428,000.

Give as You Earn (GAYE), is a *payroll giving scheme* where an employee or pensioner can donate to any charitable organisation in the UK, straight from their pay.

... at Bristol University[171]

Volunteering activities: The university has agreed that all University staff may take an additional day of paid leave each year to enable staff to participate in volunteering activities.

Public duties: The university recognises that it has a civic responsibility to allow staff to take on public duties.

Volunteer Reserve Forces: The university grants, in addition to the normal leave entitlement, five days leave with pay for employees who are required to attend training exercises, summer camps etc.

Other volunteer activities are encouraged, like assisting with reading in schools or serving as a trustee of a local community group.

---

[169] Work and Family Connection (2005). *The Most Important Work-Life-Related Studies.* Minnetonka, MN: Work and Family Connection.
[170] GSK Website; http://www.gsk.com/community/employee_involvement.htm.
[171] University of Bristol; http://www.bris.ac.uk.

... *at* *Sodexo*[172]

Sodexo has made fighting hunger the central focus of its community service efforts. Through the Stop Hunger Initiatives, staff are encouraged to participate in: *food delivery and donations* to help food banks; *job training* programs that provide economically disadvantaged adults with the job skills they need to achieve self-sufficiency; *housing* that offers affordable housing to low-income families, so that people do not have to make a choice between rent or food; *research and public policy* to support the lives of the hungry through independent non-partisan research on hunger issues; *feeding our future*, sponsoring summer lunches for children who might otherwise go hungry; *Sodexo Servathon* where employees join forces to fundraise, collect and donate food and serve meals to those in need.

Culture fit

The idea of culture fit is essential to link culture, motivation and performance: empirical evidence demonstrates that strong organisational cultures contribute to performance, provided this culture is strategically appropriate, i.e. 'fits' the needs of the organisation and of the marketplace.[173] The better the cultural fit, the better the organisation will perform.

The notion of culture fit highlights the fact that fundamentally there is not 'one best' culture. Organisations have personalities and possess a unique character that distinguishes them from one another; it is their capacity to appropriately match the specific needs of staff and the marketplace, together with their ability to adapt its behaviour, and structures and systems to those changing needs that contribute to their success. Google has created a fun, unique culture that values the unconventional approach; this is reflected in the importance of innovation in the business model.

---

[172]Sodexo Employee Handbook, March 2009; http://www.iamsodexo.com/front_en/Images/Final09HandbookE_tcm80-279403.pdf.
[173]Kotter, JP and J Heskett (1992). *Corporate Culture and Performance*. London: Free Press.

5.6.3.   *Interpersonal Relations*

> '*I am human and I need to belong, just like everybody else does.*'
>
> *Morrissey*

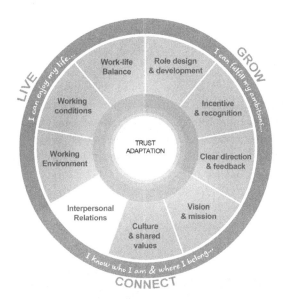

An environment where employees experience camaraderie, where productive and collaborative relationships are fostered, and where people feel a sense of belonging, can have a positive impact on individual satisfaction and organisational performance. The relationship with the fellow employees, clients and partners of the organisation form the basis of these connections.

Definition of Interpersonal Relations:

The personal connection that people feel with those they work with, whether it is the client, fellow-workers or the manager.

Relationship with direct manager

A Gallup study has found that the most important factor in whether or not employees choose to stay in a job is the quality of their working relationship with their direct superiors.[174] Other studies have also determined that a

---

[174]Schwartz, T (2009). *The Way We Are Working Isn't Working.* New York: Simon & Schuster.

primary factor in employee's satisfaction and loyalty to that employer is the employee's relationship with his or her immediate supervisor.[175]

> *'Bosses who ignore and stomp on their subordinates' humanity sometimes generate quick gains. But in the long run, such short-sightedness undermines creativity, efficiency, and commitment'*
>
> – *McKinsey*[176]

A Gallup study reveals that two million employees at 700 companies rate having a caring boss higher than money or fringe benefits. This study confirms findings by a 1999 Lou Harris Assoc.-Spherion study that found 40% of employees who rated their supervisors as poor were likely to leave their company, compared to 11% who rated them as excellent.[177]

Many studies show that for more than 75% of employees, dealing with their immediate boss, is the most stressful part of the job. A 2009 Swedish study tracking 3,122 men for 10 years found that those with bad bosses suffered 20% to 40% more heart attacks than those with good bosses.[178]

Zoom on ... The Impact of the Direct Manager

Just as the studies above note the pivotal role of the manager in maintaining employee satisfaction, other studies too highlight the key role the manager can play in impacting performance.

Today, the Internet is an oft-used forum for venting discontent against 'bad bosses'. BossRater.com allows users to give their supervisors a grade, from A to F, on such traits as honesty and trustworthiness. At eBossWatch.com, America's worst and best bosses are listed, and can be searched and rated. The site allows people to anonymously rate their current or former bosses using an evaluation form so that job seekers can size up prospective employers.[179]

---

[175]Wagner, SE (2006). Staff retention: From 'satisfied' to 'engaged'. *Nursing Management*, 37(3), 24–29.

[176]Sutton, RI (2010). Why good bosses tune in to their people. *McKinsey Quarterly*, August 2010.

[177]Work and Family Connection (2005). *The Most Important Work-Life-Related Studies*. Minnetonka, MN: Work and Family Connection.

[178]Sutton, RI (2010). Why good bosses tune in to their people. *McKinsey Quarterly*, August, pp. 1–11.

[179]'Preventing Maltweetment' (28 May 2010). *BusinessWeek*.

Connection with colleagues

Camaraderie in the workplace — to have good, productive relationships with fellow employees — is an important factor contributing to satisfaction for most people (Figure 5.8). Today, we spend more time in work and the relationships we forge with those we work with have an important human value. People by nature seek to forge bonds and with others near them, described as a yen rooted in the tribal communities of our ancestors by Kent Bailey, a professor emeritus of psychology at Virginia Commonwealth University. Today, by necessity, more people build those bonds with non-relatives; people spend more time at work and find these 'psychological kin' in the workplace.[180]

Zoom on... The Importance of Workplace Friendships

While friendships don't appear on balance sheets, they're showing up in research on the underpinnings of productivity. In 28 studies of a total of more than 105,000 employees, the Gallup Organisation found that, 'having a best friend at work' was one of the 13 employee circumstances most likely to signal a highly productive workplace — right up there with 'knowing what's expected of me' and 'having the materials and equipment I need'.[181]

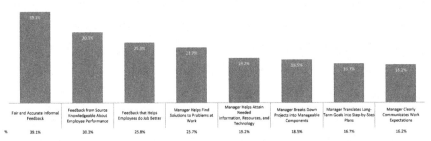

	Fair and Accurate Informal Feedback	Feedback from Source Knowledgeable About Employee Performance	Feedback that Helps Employees do Job Better	Manager Helps Find Solutions to Problems at Work	Manager Helps Attain Needed Information, Resources, and Technology	Manager Breaks Down Projects into Manageable Components	Manager Translates Long-Term Goals into Step-by-Step Plans	Manager Clearly Communicates Work Expectations
%	39.1%	30.3%	25.8%	23.7%	19.2%	18.5%	16.7%	16.2%

Figure 5.8 Percentage of impact of manager — employee interactions on employee performance.

---

180 Along with benefits and pay, employees seek friends on the job (20 February 2002). *Wall Street Journal*; http://www.mail-archive.com/futurework@scribe.uwaterloo.ca/msg02573.html.

181 The research is documented in *First, Break All the Rules*, the best-selling book by Marcus Buckingham and Curt Coffman.

Best Practices Case Study: Southwest Airlines

Fostering a sense of camaraderie and belongingness at work

Southwest Airlines began a tradition, championed by Colleen Barrett, to encourage employees to bring a sense of their true self into their workplace. 'We want to see the real you . . . we want people to have their true identity in the workplace,' says Colleen Barrett. Employees were encouraged to 'be themselves' and to share their lives outside of work through photographs; today the walls are adorned with photographs and employees express their pride in the forged values. An important goal of the photographs was the idea of celebrating success and fostering a sense of sharing and camaraderie amongst colleagues.

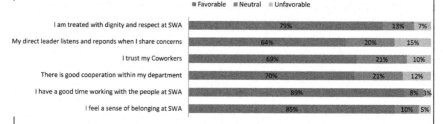

Interpersonal relations at Southwest Airlines.

The walls of photographs undoubtedly remind people of the good times they have spent together. And furthermore, studies have also demonstrated the effect of 'taking a trip down memory lane' on psychological well-being. Golden memories can also 'inoculate against future bad moods'. Much research has been found to support the notion that indulging in nostalgic thoughts makes people feel more confident of the support of their friends and family. In 2006, a team of researchers conducted an experiment on how nostalgia affects psychological well-being and it was found that it breeds happier moods and stimulates positive feelings of social integration and belongingness. It was found to have a 'social-glue' effect. 'Basking in memories elevates mood, increases self-esteem and strengthens relationships'.[182]

---

[182] *Scientific American Mind*, July/August 2010.

Zoom on ... The Impact of Social Media on Worker Relations

Social media has become ubiquitous both at work and home. Twitter users create 50 million tweets each day, and Facebook has more than 400 million users worldwide. With the number of users booming, human resource experts say an employee 'airing dirty laundry' about work could negatively impact relations at work.

A Nielson report found users dedicated about five-and-a-half hours a week on social networking sites such as Facebook and Twitter in December 2009, up 82% from the prior year.[183]

Brian Uzzi, a professor of leadership at the Kellogg School of Management at Northwestern University, notes that managers have a duty to ensure that certain comments that employees post on social media do not offend other colleagues.[184]

Teams

The size of an organisation and the structure of management within an organisation necessarily impact the relationship distance and motivational practices within the company. Many small organisations may have limitations in terms of the benefits and compensation they can offer their employees, and in many cases, the managers can be stretched and cannot offer the same attention to employees; however, an organisation that values the employees in spite of the constraints will benefit from a sustained level of commitment and motivation.

A small start-up or family run company that creates a defining culture where employees are valued and engaged often struggles to sustain this culture as the company grows in size; economies of scale and attempts to increase organisational efficiencies often lead to a more mechanistic structure and a greater distance in relationships between staff and management.[185]

Frederick Herzberg identified the distance in relationships in the organisation as an influential factor of motivation; he argued that decreasing

---

[183] *Nielsen Wire*, January 22, 2010; http://blog.nielsen.com/nielsenwire/global/led-by-facebook-twitter-global-time-spent-on-social-media-sites-up-82-year-over-year/.

[184] Chen, S (2010). Workplace rants on social media are headache for companies; CNN http://edition.cnn.com/2010/LIVING/05/12/social.media.work.rants/?hpt=Mid.

[185] Dhawan, R (2001). Firm size and productivity differential: Theory and evidence from a panel of U.S. firms. *Journal of Economic Behavior and & Organization*, March, pp. 269–293.

relationship distances by allowing employees to report directly to the recipient of the work is an effective method of encouraging motivation and commitment to the to the task.[186] Walmart was once known for the close-knit culture and a high level of engagement amongst staff despite relatively low levels of pay. However, following the exponential growth in the business, there has been a considerable rise in employee dissatisfaction.

Teams are increasingly becoming a primary means by which employees in organisations conduct work.[187] Studies demonstrate that good team cohesiveness improves member satisfaction, lowers absenteeism and lowers attrition from the group.[188]

Zoom on ... Team Efficiency at Canon

Canon improved its production process by converting all assembly lines at 54 plants in 23 countries to manufacturing cells in which teams of workers performed several different tasks to produce a finished product. This process entrusts responsibility to the teams to adjust the production output according to their estimation and this leads to increases in individual proficiency. It has improved worker satisfaction through greater camaraderie and enhancing the feeling of achievement that the workers associate with the successful and autonomous completion of a product.[189]

Connection with clients

The connections people have with clients on a daily basis can have a strong impact on people's happiness, particularly for those in the service industry. The relationships, interaction and feedback from clients can also be a source of recognition and can contribute to well-being.

---

[186]William, PJ, KB Robertson and F Herzberg (1969). Job enrichment pays off. *Harvard Business Review*, 47(2), 61–78.

[187]Guzzo, RA and GR Shea (1992). Group performance and intergroup relations in organizations. In *Handbook of Industrial and Organizational Psychology*, MD Dunnette and LM Hough (eds.), Vol. 3, pp. 269–313. Palo Alto, CA: Consulting Psychologists Press.

[188]Barsade, SG *et al.* (2000). To your heart's content: A model of affective diversity in top management teams. *Administrative Science Quarterly*, December, pp. 1191–1202.

[189]Canon Global Corporate Info; http://www.canon.com/about/activities/production.html.

Best Practices Case Study: Southwest Airlines

Client Connections

Colleen Barrett, President Emeritus of Southwest Airlines, told a story of one customer who has been flying Southwest for years: 'Because of the high frequency service, people commute to work with us and they get so they know the flight attendants that fly the same routes. Every Monday morning this customer commutes and goes back on the evening service on a Friday. Monday morning he brings the entire station and the flight attendant continental breakfast. On Friday he buys beer for the whole airplane.' According to Colleen, the connections that are forged with employees are extremely rewarding, both for employees and for customers.[190]

---

[190]Interview with Colleen Barrett, August 30, 2010.

Chapter 6

MOTIVATION IS THE KEY TO PERFORMANCE DEVELOPMENT

The success of any organisation depends on how well its employees perform at work, and this performance at work depends on different factors. People seek much more purpose, meaning and growth from work than merely compensation, and the motivation to live, grow and connect is appropriate for the development of the organisation as well as the individual. The two should go hand in hand. For organisations to compete in the complex market increasing productivity does not suffice; firms need to innovate in all aspects of the business in order to compete. Unlocking the creativity and ingenuity of the workforce plays a decisive role in the stimulation of innovation and the performance of the organisation.

> *'The strength of the team is each individual member... the strength of each member is the team.'*
>
> *Coach Phil Jackson,*
> *Los Angeles Lakers*

Organisations can be described as 'orderly arrangements of individual human interactions'.[1] Thus the link between organisational performance and individual motivation seems to be self-evident; if individuals are highly motivated, they will perform better.

Both studies and evidence have demonstrated the link between motivation and organisational performance. However, there is a difficulty in measuring the direct link between the two constructs, the problem lying

---

[1] Tannenbaum, TS (1962). *Administrative Science Quarterly.*

in the fact that many other factors may well contribute to performance. Despite the absence of an accurate measurement tool, organisations routinely attest that a positive approach to motivating people leads to improved performance and an increase in the bottom line.

The failure of rigidly 'controlled' systems of motivation, such as Frederick Taylor's scientific management, is demonstrative of the incompatibility of such negative approaches with human nature. People generally need much more than mere compensation in order to be satisfied, motivated and to remain with the organisation. At the time of Taylorism, maximising productivity and economies of scale were the chief factors contributing to the competitive advantage of a company; since then, technology and advances in machinery have changed the parameters of competitive advantage and made the necessity to drive workers to continually improve manufacturing productivity redundant in most Western economies.

Today's organisations face far greater challenges than the singular factor of increasing productivity. They need to innovate. They are dealing with intangibles such as service as well as tangible products. They are expected to behave in a caring and responsible way towards all of the stakeholders of the organisation. As Michael Porter remarks, 'Governments, activists, and the media have become adept at holding companies to account for the social consequences of their activities[2].' Organisations need internal flexibility by means of an agile, responsive workforce, in order to anticipate and match the evolving needs and values of marketplaces and even of society. The potential of people to influence the competitive positioning of the organisation is more powerful than ever because, in the 'people economy', it is the human factor that can make the difference. As Herb Kelleher, co-founder of Southwest Airlines, confirms, 'the hardest thing for a competitor to do is to copy our people... the intangibles are more important than the tangibles'. Indeed, the potential of a motivated workforce to play a strategic role in organisational success is evident.

6.1.   Understanding the Link between Motivation and Performance

The success of any organisation depends on how well its employees perform at work, and how such performance depends on different factors.

---

[2]Porter, M and M Kramer (2006). Strategy and society: The link between corporate responsibility and competitive responsibility. *Harvard Business Review*, 84(12), 78–92, 163.

Human resources play a decisive role in designing jobs, selecting the right candidates and providing training to ensure a correct fit beween people and jobs. Managers need to appreciate individual differences to ensure employees are well motivated to work. A positive working environment and a healthy organisational culture are conducive to ensuring a highly motivated workforce leading to organisational success.

6.1.1. *Performance is Dependent on a Number of Other Factors that Support Motivation*

Motivation (the desire to do the job), ability (the capability to do the job) and resources (the tools, materials and information needed to do the job) act together to impact performance; for maximum performance all three factors must be high. They are inextricably intertwined — motivation tends to be higher when the individual feels his abilities are used to its full potential and actions needed to increase ability requires motivation on the employee's part in order to be successful.

Zoom on ... Performance

Performance = f(ability × motivation)

Vroom (1964) followed Maier (1955) and others in suggesting that performance can be a multiplicative function of motivation: [Performance = f(ability × motivation)]. This formulation has been widely adopted.

Variances were suggested to better account for resources. Melvin Blumberg and Charles Pringle, for instance, proposed a three-dimensional interactive model where Capacity (ability, age, health, knowledge, skills...), Willingness (motivation, job satisfaction, anxiety, self-image, personality...) and Opportunity (tools, equipment and supplies, working conditions, organisational policies, time...) all account for Performance.

The most successful performance improvement efforts combine strategies for improving each factor (motivation, ability and resources) and build on a supportive work environment where good motivational techniques are used on a regular basis. Diagnosis of performance issues should be prioritised to identify the root of difficulties and the springboard for improvement; then the employer and the employee can discuss and agree upon an action plan for improvement, and monitor progress. This process in itself can be a highly effective first step in addressing performance when it creates a positive environment where people feel supported to reach their performance potential.

Do performance problems come from lack of ability or low motivation? It is important to make sure that people match their job in the first place because if the real issue is ability, then motivational practices cannot be efficient: do employees have what they need to perform well and meet expectations? Do they need additional training? Are there parts of the jobs that need to be redesigned or reassigned? Individual ability to perform can be managed through the selection process, providing adequate training and ensuring a right fit between the ability to perform and job description.

Assuming the organisation takes care of this dimension, it does not ensure that the individuals give their best continuously on the job. Motivation is crucial to put in the required effort in doing the job, which explains the different work behaviours of people who are equally qualified. Managers need to find out what motivates workers by looking at their behaviour and discussing with them. The final 'recipe' from the mix of motivational strategies will vary from workplace situation to situation and be dependant on the corporate policy of the organisation.

People's motivation in itself should be carefully managed. Motivated individuals will perform well provided they spend their energy on aspects of the work that are effectively aimed at benefitting the company. Special attention should be paid to work pressure too; motivation has to be balanced in order to avoid too much stress, which can be harmful in both the short and the long term.

6.1.2. *Satisfaction also Plays a Role for Sustained Motivation*

Employees who are motivated to strive for organisational goals and to exert discretionary effort are those that are willing to go the 'extra mile', to go above and beyond what is asked of them. Herzberg's research identified the importance of both satisfaction and motivation. He highlighted the possibility that an employee who is satisfied with the conditions of pay and the working environment will not feel the need to leave the organisation, but is not likely to be motivated to contribute beyond the parameters of the role. The optimal situation is when an employee feels happy with the conditions and the working environment, but also feels motivated over the long term. An employee who is experiencing high motivation in combination with high satisfaction is the most valuable to the company and will help contribute to the success of the organisation.

High Motivation Low Satisfaction		High Motivation High Satisfaction	
Employees will be motivated to achieve goals in the short-term but dissatisfaction with conditions means there is a high risk of turnover.	Not Sustainable	Employees willingly strive to achieve organisational goals and are committed to personal and organisational success. Low risk of turnover.	Optimal for sustainable motivation
Low Motivation Low Satisfaction		Low Motivation High Satisfaction	
These employees are not likely to strive for organisational goals, nor speak well about the company. High risk of turnover.	Least valuable situation	Employees are satisfied with conditions and comfortable in the organisation but are not energised to strive for personal and organisational success. Low risk of turnover.	Sustainable but low level of discretionary effort

6.2. In What Way Does Motivation Impact Performance?

A contented motivated workforce leads to higher and better quality performance, profitability, greater levels of sustainable productivity, lower turnover and absenteeism, and a more reactive workforce that can innovate and respond to the needs of the organisation or the market.

6.2.1. *Productivity: Happy to Achieve*

Employee productivity depends on the amount of time an individual is physically present at a job and also the degree to which he or she is 'mentally present' or efficiently functioning while present at a job.[3] A 2007 Towers Perrin survey of nearly 90,000 employees worldwide found that companies with low levels of employee engagement had a 33% annual decline in operating income and a 11% annual drop in earnings growth. On the other hand, those with high engagement reported a 19% increase in operating income and a 28% increase in earnings per share.[4]

In Southwest Airlines, a higher level of staff productivity is one of the determinants of the success of their low-cost business model. According to Colleen Barrett, 'Although our wages are consistent with those in the rest of the industry, we seem to get a lot more effort from our workers.' The Southwest passenger-to-employee ratio of 2,100 to 1 is about twice the average of their nearest competitor; this translates into 91 people to run each plane, far outpacing the other major airlines for productivity. Yet, customer service does not suffer at Southwest; it is quite the opposite in fact. Barrett adds, 'Customer letters praise our service and often single out particular employees for their humor, creativity, and endearingly helpful ways. In our case, it really does seem that less is more'.

6.2.2. *Service Quality: Happy to Help*

A study by the Forum for People Performance Management at Northwestern University in Evanston confirms that happy employees — even the ones who never see a client — impact customer satisfaction, and customer satisfaction in turn directly effects financial performance: 'When employees are engaged — satisfied and challenged — you have customers who score high on satisfaction and are more committed and loyal'. Mulhern believes most companies don't do enough to motivate outside their sales forces when he states, 'The sales team tends to get a lot of the attention because it's the most visible, but behind every sales team is a support staff and behind that support staff is a human resources department, a marketing department and

---

[3]Goetzel, RZ and RJ Ozminkowski (1999). Health productivity management assists benefits business strategy. *Employee Benefit News.*
[4]Insights from Towers Watson's 2010 Global Workforce Study. The New Employment Deal: How Far, How Fast and How Enduring.

so on. All employees need to be aware of the corporate goals and need to be attuned to keeping the brand's promise to clients.'

At Southwest Airlines, a commitment to employee satisfaction is acknowledged as an important determinant of the quality of effort by employees. The company has been tracking complaints and service commendations according to each station over the years and they have identified a correlation between employee satisfaction and the quality of the customer service. One station had a small number of staff but had always been 'in the top three for commendations' by customers. A drop in customer commendations and a rapid rise in customer complaints were swiftly perceived by the head office and a call was made to get to the bottom of the issue. The problem was quickly identified as the result of a newly appointed supervisor with an overly zealous and pompous disposition who was making life unpleasant for the 30 or so staff with whom he was dealing in the station. Apparently 'the title went to his head and he wants to show who is boss', reported one member of staff. The issue was resolved but the lessons were not forgotten: the line manager has a potent impact on staff morale, and equally, staff morale has a direct impact on customer service standards.[5]

Zoom on... Studies Linking Employee Satisfaction with Productivity, Performance and Customer Satisfaction

In 1997, Development Dimensions International (DDI) conducted focus groups, customer interviews, literature reviews and surveys to determine drivers of an effective service environment. DDI found evidence of a 'circular relationship' between employee satisfaction and retention, and customer satisfaction and loyalty, and increases in company profitability. In addition, employee satisfaction was strongly related to employee commitment and loyalty, and both measures have proven relationships to retention and productivity.[6]

In *The Service Profit Chain* (1997), the authors proposed a model that workforce capability, satisfaction and loyalty would lead to customers' perceptions of value. Value perception would lead to customer satisfaction and loyalty, which would lead to profits and growth. The study

---

[5]Interview with Colleen Barrett, President Emeritus of Southwest Airlines, 30 August 2010.

[6]Author Unknown (1997). An effective service environment, *Managers Handbook*, May.

found that employees' perceptions of their capabilities, satisfaction and length-of-service correlated with customer satisfaction.[7]

Gallup reports that highly satisfied groups of employees often exhibit above-average levels of the following characteristics:

Customer loyalty (56%)
Productivity (50%)
Employee retention (50%)
Safety records (50%)
Profitability (33%)

A Watson Wyatt Worldwide study found that the practice of maintaining a collegial, flexible workplace is associated with the second largest increase in shareholder value (a 9% gain), suggesting that employee satisfaction is directly related to financial gain.[8]

Over 40% of the companies listed in the top 100 of *Fortune* magazine's 'America's Best Companies to Work For' also appear on the *Fortune 500*. While it is possible that employees enjoy working at these organisations because they are successful, the Watson Wyatt Worldwide Human Capital Index study suggests that effective human resources practices lead to positive financial outcomes more often than positive financial outcomes lead to good practices.[9]

6.2.3. *Innovation: Happy to Create*

> *'The need to innovate quickly is becoming more important to business.'*
>
> *Robert Whiteside*

Motivating staff to actively innovate to transform the business can be a powerful determinant of business success. A study of 3,500 employees, 100 HR managers and 100 IT managers across the UK, France, Germany, the United States and Japan, conducted by the Future Foundation on behalf of

[7]Koys, DJ (2001). The effects of employee satisfaction, organizational citizenship behavior, and turnover on organizational effectiveness: A unit-level, longitudinal study, *Personnel Psychology*, 54, 101–114. Heskett JL, *et al.* (1994). Putting the service-profit chain to work, *Harvard Business Review*, March–April, pp. 164–174.

[8]Author Unknown, Human Capital Index: Human Capital as a Lead Indicator of Shareholder Value, *Watson Wyatt Worldwide*. (Available through www.watsonwyatt.com.)

[9]Author Unknown, America's Top Employers, *Fortune* (2002). (Available through www.fortune.com.)

Google, found an 81% positive correlation between employee collaboration and innovation across all markets.

In the UK, employees who are given the opportunity to collaborate at work are nearly twice as likely to have contributed new ideas to their companies. HR need to ensure employees are motivated to collaborate and innovate, with the study finding that 34% of HR personnel agree they need to learn new skills to foster a sense of corporate community and one-third of chief information officers believing they will take on more responsibility for innovation in the future. This is important for the culture of the business, how to incentivise and reward ideas and innovation, where and how work is performed and policies and practices around social networking. 'The need to innovate quickly is becoming more important to business', says Robert Whiteside, Google head of enterprise UK, Ireland and Benelux. In Google, employees actively contribute to innovation in the organisation and are encouraged and rewarded for this behavior.

6.2.4. *Loyalty: Happy to Stay*

One of the advantages of fostering a good level of employee motivation throughout the organisation is the impact on retention: happy, motivated people are less likely to leave an organisation than those lacking opportunities and motivation.

A survey commissioned by Investors in People found that 43% of respondents are considering leaving their job in the next 12 months, largely as a result of being demotivated in their current role. Nearly half of respondents (44%) said their employer has failed to continue supporting their career development beyond their initial induction period, while three in ten said they felt unsupported by their managers.

A study by the Society for Human Resource Management found that three out of four U.S. workers are actively looking for a new job. Similar numbers were found by Salary.com, which surveyed 14,000 workers to discover that 65% were launching some sort of job search.[10]

The organisations that top the best place to work lists often have much lower rates of staff attrition. Google's annual staff attrition remains 'extraordinarily low' at 4%. The national average was 29.3% in 2005 for companies in the information industry.[11] It is not simply a case of creating a fun and creative working environment; employees in Google

---

[10]In 'Workers' loyalty to employers rising, survey finds.' On HR News at SHRM.org, 21 November 2005.
[11]U.S. Bureau of Labor Statistics (2005).

Figure 6.1   Reasons for leaving job (sample 1000).

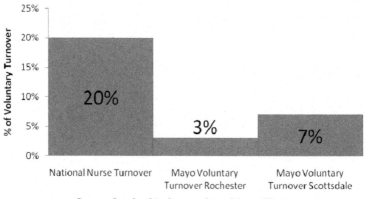

Source: Leadership lessons from Mayo Clinic.

Figure 6.2   Voluntary turnover levels at Mayo Clinic versus national level.

are given opportunities to grow and connect with each other and with the organisational strategy and goals. Employees contribute directly to the success of the business. People are eager to work at Google and applications to job openings are exceedingly high (approximately 1,300 resumes a day).[12]

Mayo Clinic, too, has an extraordinarily low level of employee attrition relative to other hospitals in the United States. Mayo Clinic ranked 55 on the 13th annual '100 Best Companies to Work For' in 2010. Whereas the national hospital nurse turnover rate hovers around 20%, voluntary turnover for Mayo hospital nurses in 2003 was about 3% at Rochester and

---

[12]Great Place to Work® Institute (2007). Why Google is Number One.

about 7% at Scottsdale (a more competitive recruiting market). Voluntary physician turnover rates in 2003 were less than 4% on both campuses.[13]

According to John H. Noseworthy, MD, President and CEO, 'I'm often asked what sets Mayo Clinic apart. The answer is complex, involving our history, our teamwork and our long-standing commitment to excellence. But put simply, we feel our people — and their approach to patient care — distinguish Mayo Clinic.'[14]

6.3. Motivation at Work is a Mutually Beneficial Relationship

'Unless both sides win, no agreement can be made permanent.'

Jimmy Carter

6.3.1. *A Win-Win Value Exchange*

There is a vast difference between an employee who decides to put in a 'transactional' effort at work, to give the minimum possible effort for an agreed sum of money, with an employee who feels motivated and inspired to contribute to the growth of the organisation, to think creatively, to connect with others in the organisation, and to put forth his best effort. There is a fundamental value exchange between an employer and an employee, composed of both tangible and intangible factors, that goes beyond the compensation and effort exchange. An employee may work for an agreed salary but all of the other factors such as opportunities for growth and development, interest and challenge in the role, the sense of connection with the organisation and with co-workers, and the quality of the working environment, will contribute to an employee's sense of value. An employee who sees these factors as contributing to personal goals and providing a sense of achievement, accomplishment or competence will be motivated to reciprocate with an effort that reflects this value.

> *'There is an old saying you can take a horse to the water but you cannot force it to drink; it will drink only if it's thirsty — so with people. They will do what they want to do or otherwise motivated to do.'*
>
> *V.H. Vroom*

---

[13]Berry, L and K Seltman (2008). *Management Lessons from Mayo Clinic*. New York: McGraw Hill, p. 142.

[14]Mayo Clinic Website; http://www.mayoclinic.org/about/noseworthy-message.html.

The 'psychological contract' refers to the relationship between an employer and its employees, and specifically concerns mutual expectations of inputs and outcomes. The concept was introduced in 1960 by Argyris. It received little attention thereafter until the 1990s when the economic downturn led to restructuring, downsizing, mergers and takeovers in many organisations. These circumstances were accompanied by changes in how personnel felt and acted towards their employers.[15]

Psychological contracts can be defined as 'the beliefs individuals hold regarding the terms and conditions of the exchange agreement between themselves and their organisations'.[16] This takes the employees' ideas about what they expect from the employer and what they feel they owe to the organisation into account. 'The psychological contract' is an increasingly relevant aspect of workplace relationships and is very useful in understanding better how to align people's needs with those of the organisation.

Motivation at work is a winning combination for performance: organisations commit to employee satisfaction and engagement and are expected to provide resources and opportunities for achievement; employees commit to high performance for the success of the organisation, by accomplishing their tasks and contributing to the organisation's growth on a daily basis. Motivation at work is about creating a workplace where employees want to stay, grow and contribute their experience and expertise in a mutually beneficial relationship. And finally, the relationship between motivation and performance can in fact be a mutually reinforcing one: high motivation leads to higher and better quality performance, and consequently better performance leads to a higher sense of achievement and result in greater motivation.

---

[15] Van de Ven, C (date unknown). The Psychological Contract; a Big Deal? , Behavioural Sciences Service Centre, Ministry of Defence, The Hague, Netherlands.
[16] Rousseau, DM (1995). *Psychological Contracts in Organizations: Understanding Written and Unwritten Agreements.* Thousand Oaks, CA: Sage Publications.

Chapter 7

CONCLUSION

7.1. Valuing People to Create Value: An Innovative Approach to Leveraging Motivation At Work

A universally accepted understanding in business today is that people play an integral role in the success of the organisation. Yet, the challenge lies in the fact that motivation, by its very nature, is an unstable condition. It is essentially an energised human behaviour, and thus it is susceptible to transition and variance, and likely to dwindle or develop over time, depending on the goals of the individual and the desire to achieve these goals. Inspiring and maintaining employee motivation at work thus has a strong impact on company performance. Motivation at work necessitates one key parameter: individual behavior must be directed towards the achievement of organisational goals; otherwise, it is of little value to the organisation.

Yet, it does not suffice to consider only the goals of the organisation for individual motivation to be unrelenting and sustainable. The shortcoming of Taylorism, or 'scientific management', is attributed to the very fact that motivating people to increase productivity was calculated with a myopic disregard for individual needs. People, it transpired, are not happy to be treated like cogs in a machine. Consequentially, many of the theoretical meanderings over the past century are somewhat of an antidote to the coercive approach of Taylorism.[17] All of the theorists, in one way or another,

---

[17] Won-joo, Yun and F Mulhern (2009). Leadership and the performance of people in organizations: Enriching employees and connecting people, *Forum for People Performance Management and Measurement Publication*, November.

have crusaded for the consideration of the human perspective when seeking to inspire motivation at work. Maslow developed a hierarchy of the needs that lie at the root of human behaviour and drive motivation. Vroom put forward the idea that the personal value an individual associates with the outcome of a task at work is instrumental in his choice to complete that task. Herzberg asserted that by making work meaningful, and giving people opportunities to realise their aspirations, people will take a vested interest in their work, an essential parameter for sustainable motivation. Thus it can be concluded from the theoretical foundations that an understanding of what the individual values at work, and aligning these goals with those of the organisation, is essential for motivated behaviour at work to have a mutual benefit for the organisation and the individual.

7.1.1.   *Motivation at Work Plays an Essential Role in Organisational Success*

Organisations face greater challenges today than ever before: creating economies of scale, increasing productivity and innovating within the fierce competitive environment of a globalised marketplace. People in the organisation are being asked to do more with less, while being creative and innovative in how they work. Smart, focused motivation is central to a company's success. This is why a people-focused perspective is evident in many of today's most successful organisations. In the contemporary dynamic economy, where firms are battling for the same market space, organisations have to continually reinvent who they are and what they do in both large and small ways. The ability to innovate and to adapt creatively to the competitive environment can only be achieved through the reactivity, agility and creativity of the people in the organisation.[18] As Peter Drucker states, 'No company, non-profit, or government agency can prevent a major catastrophe, but you can build an organisation that is battle-ready, that has high morale that knows how to behave, that trusts itself and where people trust one another.'[19] Thus, cultivating the positive motivation of the people in the organisation has become an increasingly strategic factor in leveraging business success.

---

[18]McDonough, EF, MH Zach, H-E Lin and I Berdrow (2008). Integrating innovation style and knowledge into strategy. *MIT Sloan Management Review*, 50, 53–58.
[19]Drucker, PF (1999). *Management Challenges for the 21st Century*. New York: Harper Business.

Likewise, the side-effects of our fast-paced environment can take its toll on well-being. Unless organisations take precautions against the symptoms, they suffer the consequences of individual burnout, stress or illness. Management that thrives on fear or punitive action can create a barrier to the creativity and motivation of its people. Andy Pearson, once voted 'toughest boss in America' and considered 'brutally abrasive' as a leader, realised that this fear-induced motivation was limiting the potential of the people in the organisation: 'If I could only unleash the power of everybody in the organisation, instead of just a few people, what could we accomplish? We'd be a much better company.' This realisation stimulated a reversal in his leadership style to become a leader that instead emphasised positive guidance, as opposed to rigid control.[20] A people-centric approach is more appropriate for the emerging knowledge and services economy.[21]

The most successful organisations are looking after the well-being of their employees, giving them a voice, listening to their individual needs, respecting and reciprocating the value that they bring to the organisation, and thereby unlocking the untapped value that they stand to bring. This positive approach goes hand-in-hand with organisational success; as John Noseworthy, MD, President and CEO of Mayo Clinic, states 'I'm often asked what sets Mayo Clinic apart. The answer is complex, involving our history, our teamwork and our long-standing commitment to excellence. But put simply, we feel our people — and their approach to patient care — distinguish Mayo Clinic.'[22]

7.1.2. *Bridging the Gap between Individual Motivation and Organisational Performance*

There are three key drivers upon which the firms that we have researched have developed motivation in the organisation; we have classified these drivers as Live, Grow and Connect. Underpinning these three drivers are the central values of Trust and Adapt. Henry Mintzberg has underlined the importance of developing 'trust' in the organisation, a culture where the values of 'caring about our work, our colleagues, and our place in the world'

---

[20]Dorset, D (2001). Andy Pearson finds love (31 July 2001). *Fast Company*; www.fastcompany.com/magazine/49/pearson.html.

[21]Won-joo, Yun and F Mulhern (2009). Leadership and the performance of people in organizations: enriching employees and connecting people, Forum for People Performance Management and Measurement Publication, November.

[22]Mayo Clinic Website; http://www.mayoclinic.org/about/noseworthy-message.html.

is cultivated. Motivation is innately unique, and functions heterogeneously from one person to the next. Thus, the importance of adapting the levers to the individual needs of the employees is central to the motivation spectrum.

'*Live*' supports the idea that work is first and foremost a means to allow people to satisfy, whether directly or indirectly, their fundamental physiological and psychological needs (shelter, security,...) and to go beyond towards greater satisfaction and well-being. Ensuring secure and fair working conditions, creating a quality working environment and helping people to balance private and professional priorities is a critical basis for employee satisfaction and motivation. People should work in a place where they actually want to come to work, which adequately facilitates the execution of their job, and is safe and convivial. The design of the workspace and the conviviality of the working environment can act as a vehicle for promoting positive attitudes and inspiring creativity. We characterise this driver as the opportunity for people to 'Live', to be able to enjoy a good quality of life.

'*Grow*' recognises the human need for competence, progress and self-achievement and to find interest and meaning in their work. Organisations that encourage a good person-role fit and provide opportunities for progression and challenge, responsibility, empowerment and growth have more committed and motivated employees. Goal-setting and feedback are other essential components for motivation, and they direct individual behavior towards the achievement of organisational goals. Incentives and recognition also play an important role in orienting, encouraging and sustaining motivation at work. In Southwest Airlines, the productivity level is much higher than other airlines, so employees clearly have to work hard. Yet, in spite of the level of effort required, the employees appear to really enjoy their work, why? Colleen Barrett describes it as thus: 'I want you to enjoy what you're doing. You don't enjoy what you're doing if you're just handing out peanuts and drinks. You enjoy it if you can be interactive, if you can have conversations, if they [customers] know your name.' We characterise this driver as the opportunity for people to 'Grow', to be able to fulfil their ambitions.

'*Connect*' relates to the fact that most people seek connections in work, whether it is with their colleagues, their leaders, the clients of the organisation or the organisation itself. People need to find purpose and meaning in their work. A cohesive, collaborative environment, where people share common values and are inspired by an overarching vision to which they contribute, helps people to 'feel at home' at work, and to invest in the goals of the organisation. The need for connection is a fundamental human need and plays an important role in creating employee satisfaction; it is also a motor of organisational success. We characterise this driver as the opportunity for people to 'Connect', to know themselves and to work in a place where they feel they belong.

There is a vast difference between an employee that decides to put in a 'transactional' effort at work, to exert the minimum possible effort for an agreed sum of money, with an employee who feels motivated and inspired to contribute to the growth of the organisation, to think creatively, to connect with others in the organisation, and to put forth his best effort. Every organisation can develop today, through the drivers of Live, Grow and Connect, a focus on the quality of life of the people in the organisation, a commitment to their future, and an investment in their well-being. The result is an agile, inspired and engaged workforce that plays an instrumental role in creating organisational value.

ABOUT THE AUTHORS

Hervé Mathe
Hervé Mathe is a Professor of Innovation and Strategy at ESSEC Business school and President of the Institute for Service Innovation and Strategy (ISIS), Chair in Innovation and Services, ISIS, the La Poste Chair in Strategic Management of Services, and the Chair in Innovation and Quality of Daily Life. He is currently the Dean of the ESSEC Asia Center in Singapore. Formerly the Director of Strategy at ESSEC, he also previously held the position of Dean of ESSEC Executive Education and postgraduate Masters division. He has served as a Visiting Professor at the Harvard Business School and the Wharton School, National University of Singapore and Victoria University of Wellington in Asia-Pacific, as well as at Bocconi University and EPFL (the Swiss Federal Institute of Technology) in Europe. Author/co-author of 11 books and more than 100 articles and chapters related to innovation, services management and the coordination of supply chains, Hervé frequently hosts roundtable discussions and research colloquiums in Europe and other parts of the world. A Bower Fellow of Harvard University, Hervé holds a doctorate from the Institut d'Etudes Politiques de Paris, a second doctorate from the Université Paris IX Dauphine, and also a PhD in technology management from Cranfield University.

Xavier Pavie
Xavier Pavie is the Director of ISIS and lecturer in innovation management and strategic marketing at ESSEC Business School. He holds a doctorate from Paris Ouest University, a masters in business science as well as a masters in philosophy. Xavier has also successfully held executive positions in leading companies for 15 years. After serving for several years as a marketing director with a particular focus on service innovation, he decided to join the academic sphere to strengthen ESSEC in the field of

innovation management. Xavier's publications emphasise philosophical approaches to innovation management as true motivational instruments for the management of change and the notion of 'responsible innovation' as a source of innovation and performance. He has published several articles and books on philosophy, including '*L'apprentissage de soi, La méditation philosophique*' (Eyrolles) and also on service innovation, such as '*Management stratégique des services et innovation: nécessité et complexité*' (L'Harmattan, 2010).

Marwyn O'Keeffe

Marwyn O'Keeffe holds a BComm Euro degree in European Commerce and French and a Masters of Science in Food Business from University College Cork (UCC). She is a Research Associate in innovation management at ISIS. She has worked as a researcher in the Food Business and Development Department in UCC in collaboration with Relay Research and University College Dublin, specialising in consumer behaviour and strategic marketing of novel foods. Prior to joining ISIS, she worked for several years in Paris as a market researcher and consultant in business development and marketing. Her current research areas of interest include the mechanisms for stimulating innovation in large service organisations and the relationship between employee well-being, motivation and performance.

INDEX